BAND-TAILED PIGEON

BAND-TAILED PIGEON

Wilderness Bird at Risk

WORTH MATHEWSON

art by
David Hagerbaumer

TIMBER PRESS
Portland · Cambridge

Frontispiece: *Dawn on the Eddyville Burn.* Watercolor by
David Hagerbaumer.

Photographs are by the author unless otherwise indicated.

Published in 2005 by
Timber Press, Inc.
The Haseltine Building
133 s.w. Second Avenue, Suite 450
Portland, Oregon 97204–3527, u.s.a.

Timber Press
2 Station Road
Swavesey
Cambridge CB4 5QJ, u.k.

www.timberpress.com

Printed in China

Library of Congress Cataloging-in-Publication Data

Mathewson, Worth, 1943–
    Band-tailed pigeon : wilderness bird at risk / Worth Mathewson ; art by
    David Hagerbaumer.
        p. cm.
    Includes bibliographical references and index.
    ISBN 0-88192-712-0 (hardcover)
    1. Band-tailed pigeon. I. Title.

    QL696.C63M28 2005
    333.95'865—dc22

                                                            2004020465

A catalog record for this book is also available from the British Library.

To those who have been involved in band-tailed pigeon research
during the past thirty years, especially those at Oregon State University.
Dr. Robert Jarvis told me during our first meeting that
"There is a lot we don't know about the bandtail;
we are going to try to learn more over the coming years."
They certainly did. The insight into the pigeon's habits
gained through their efforts has proven invaluable.
I deeply appreciate it.

Contents

Color photographs follow page 64

Preface

In late April 1956 my father, Kent Mathewson, accepted the position of city manager of Salem, Oregon. At the time we lived in the small town of Martinsville, Virginia. In taking this job my parents were faced with a monumental decision—all of our relatives on both sides of the family lived close by in North Carolina. Oregon seemed the other side of the world for our extremely interlocking southern clan. And it certainly was.

Dad told us at dinner several days prior to his official announcement to the city council. My two brothers and I were instructed sternly not to tell anyone beforehand. On or about May 1, I went to the old Martinsville Junior High School with the news of our move West. Dad was due to address the council at a noon meeting, so I was allowed to tell friends and teachers during lunch.

At the time Fred Robbins was my closest friend. I can recall very clearly standing on the steps outside the ancient brick building and telling him of the move. But much more important, I can remember what else I said. I told him that I would be able to see the band-tailed pigeon in Oregon.

That I knew of the band-tailed pigeon while living several thousand miles east of its range was not by coincidence. At age four I had begun collecting bird cards that came in Arm & Hammer baking soda boxes. At age six I asked for and received a copy of *Birds of America*, the classic 1917 work edited by T. Gilbert Pearson, then president of the National Association of Audubon Societies. The dust jacket pictured a red-tailed and a Cooper's hawk perched on a dead snag above an Appalachian-appearing backdrop. The artist was Louis Agassiz Fuertes.

The book made a deep impression on me then and still does today. *Birds of America* is still my favorite book on birds—and I have a lot of them. After acquiring it my parents took turns reading it to me, generally a few chapters at a time. When I reached the age that I could read it myself, I did, time and time again. By 1956, when I was twelve, I had nearly memorized most of the text including, of course, the short chapter on the band-tailed pigeon written by William L. Finley, Oregon's turn-of-the-century wildlife photographer and writer.

Fred Robbins was always mature for his age. He spoke in a slow, deliberate manner, and if he felt something was of importance, he placed unmistakable emphasis on it. He was very measured, in other words. This was somewhat odd in contrast to his role on the Martinsville High School football team as a bruising, active 220-pound tackle. In later life he went on to a career as English professor at Southern Illinois University and editor of the school's literary magazine *Sou'wester*. He also edited this book. After I told him that the move to Oregon would enable me to see the band-tailed pigeon, Fred replied in that tone reserved for items of great significance: "You are indeed fortunate."

I was. After forty-eight years of nearly constant contact in some manner with the pigeon, I appreciate Fred's remark even more. Maybe if we had stayed in the South I would have found another bird to capture and hold my untiring interest. Likely? But while I don't generally put much store in such things, I can't help wonder if fate didn't play a part. I certainly would like to think so.

WORTH MATHEWSON 2004

From British Columbia to Peru

Somehow, perhaps because of his erratic habits, the mystery of his mountain wilderness retreats, and his wary, untrusting nature, I think of the band-tailed pigeon, or blue pigeon, or blue rock, or wild pigeon, or white-collared pigeon, as he has been variously and colloquially called over decades since we first knew him, as a most romantic bird.

BYRON DALRYMPLE 1949

THIRTY-THREE years ago, late on a cold rainy September afternoon, I was on the Campbell River on Vancouver Island, British Columbia. I was purposefully fishing the river near the home of Roderick Haig-Brown, although catching sea-run cutthroats or steelhead was the remotest thought on my mind. I made cast after cast with diminishing hopes that the greatest of all angler-naturalists would appear on the river and that we would strike up a streamside conversation. My fantasies are never instantaneous. And if they happen at all, they habitually piece themselves together over long periods of time and through many side channels of life. Roderick Haig-Brown wasn't fishing that day, and I didn't catch any trout.

I was actually on my way north to Kelsey Bay to catch the ferry the next morning to Prince Rupert, then over to the Queen Charlotte Islands to spend a few days trying to learn anything that I could of the saturation population of peregrine falcons that

For my friend Worth Mathewson
with warmest regards—
Darc N.

nest there. The adventure proved to be a memorable one. On the ferry was a counterculture, back-to-the-woodser from New Jersey with vague plans of selling his practically new jeep in Prince Rupert, then continuing north into lower coastal Alaska to homestead and build boats. Subsistence off the land appeared to be his most pressing single concern, and since it seemed I was interested in wildlife he pumped me for ideas. Somewhere in the conversation I suggested that sea gull eggs were edible, a meager, passing remark meant to be taken lightly. But that bit of information seemed to erase all apprehension for the future from his mind. He had numerous questions about where gulls nest, how easy it would be to reach the nests, the number of eggs a gull has, and whether one would need to climb trees to obtain the eggs.

His noticeable lift in spirits with the information may have been due to the setting. I offered the tip in the late evening, as the ferry passed cold, bleak shorelines and small islands and the rain hit the windows with the force and chilling effect only possible in the Far North, making the six northbound travelers that had grouped at a table perhaps a little more inclined to share our thoughts. With the quiet tone of the conversation as the group drank dark coffee, not a word was interjected to point out that sea gulls wouldn't be laying eggs again for eight months.

And there was also a wild night spent in a hotel in Prince Rupert while I waited to make contact with a fishing boat on which I hoped to hitchhike a ride out to the Charlottes. I had a room directly adjacent to the bar. The bar's patrons, all Indians, showed a remarkable lack of interest in my questions about falcons. It only took me half a beer to catch the heavy atmosphere in the air, quickly return to my room, and listen to the fight that broke out five minutes later. For added security, I wedged a chair against the doorknob. This experience strengthened my belief that bird watchers and certain strains of fly fishermen live on the far outer reaches of mainstream life.

I did, however, learn much about the peregrines of the Queen Charlottes in the following days. Principally, if I returned during the spring I could arrange for a boat and guide and quite easily find aeries and photograph the falcons. My September visit was devoted just to seeing passing birds.

But most important of all—and a memory as vivid as any on that trip—was that a few miles north of Mr. Haig-Brown's home I saw a large flock of band-tailed pigeons (*Patagioenas fasciata*) grouped on the dripping boughs of a cedar tree. I pulled the car to the narrow shoulder of the road to watch the pigeons huddle in the cold rain and wind. Those bandtails were the northernmost pigeons that I had seen.

A few years later, a group of geographers from the University of Wisconsin and I were sitting at a table outside a café on the shores of Lake Atitlan in Guatemala. Between rounds of beer, our waiter was assuring me that he was one of the leading local experts on the poc, the rare Atitlan grebe, endemic to the vast reed-bound shores of the high mountain lake. With a broad smile, coupled with exaggerated gestures of rubbing his stomach, he also informed me that he ate them at every opportunity and that they were tough but good with hot sauce.

This is the type of response that can often be heard when a visitor raises a question about any species of bird. I had run into it many times before throughout Central America. But with this fellow it bothered me. I didn't like him and suspected that he had never seen the bird. Clearly he must have felt my irritation, which made matters worse. When we asked for menus, he informed us that the special that night was grebe, prepared in a half dozen ways, and for the next hour the waiter drew all the humor he could out of his joke. But later in the evening, likely fearing for his tip, the jokes halted. He became serious and helpful. He told me that there was no need to try to obtain a boat to travel to the far shores of the lake, as the grebes could be seen in a small reed patch near a hotel only a mile away.

And at first light of dawn it was apparently true. In the chilled, clear morning light I hurriedly photographed an Atitlan grebe that paid no attention to me as it worked its way along the shore. Photographing the bird was so easy that I spent less than ten minutes behind the camera.

It was months later, back in the States, with all my film developed and viewed for the first time that I came out of my chair when the first of the grebe's images appeared on the screen. Center and shining against the blue of the lake and lush green of the reeds was the chalk white bill of a common coot, not a grebe at all. My mistake must have been the result of trying to stay even with the beer intake of the university group the previous night.

At the time, however, I was flush with the remarkably easy success. Later that day we drove back up the steep mountainous road that snakes down to the lake and continued north toward Mexico. I capitalized the day when I saw a flock of *paloma de collar*, or *pichon grande*, as the band-tailed pigeon is called in Central America. It went on record as my southernmost sighting of a bird I have grown to love on a level above nearly all others.

Years after my first visit to the Queen Charlotte Islands to view peregrines, my wife and I made three return trips. We were able to photograph the falcons on their aeries with ease. We also found large colonies of Cassin's auklets and ancient murrelets, and we marveled at these while documenting their breeding habits on small, wilderness islands. I also was able to visit Mr. Haig-Brown's home. He had passed away by then, and his widow, Ann, kindly hosted my wife and me during a visit. When I told her of my fishing the Campbell near their home in hope of meeting him, she said she wished I would have just knocked on the door, as I was the type of person he would have enjoyed talking with, rather than some who came to call in increasing numbers late in his life.

My northern and southern sightings of the band-tailed pigeon are very close to the limits of their known range. The extreme northern range for the pigeon appears to be the Queen Charlotte Islands and the adjacent mainland, with a few rare sightings recorded in southern Alaska. As a breeding bird, the band-tailed pigeon is common from central Vancouver Island and mainland western British Columbia south to about San Francisco. The largest breeding population is found in Oregon. The two mountain ranges that run unbroken for this distance provide the sharp geographical borders of the pigeon's range. The bulk of the far western bandtails breed in the Coast Range of British Columbia, Washington, Oregon, and northern California, which rises from the beaches of the Pacific. To the east the Cascade Mountains form an almost uniform border; except in a few isolated pockets, bandtails are found only on the western slopes of the Cascades in British Columbia, Washington, and Oregon and the Sierra Nevada in California.

I did once see a woefully misplaced individual of the Pacific race of bandtail in the vast sagebrush expanse near Malheur National Wildlife Refuge in eastern Oregon. The word near has a very important significance here. The pigeon was settled on top of a sagebrush just a half mile past the old settlement of The Narrows, which today is just one small ranch. The turn down to the refuge headquarters is just past The Narrows. If you don't make this turn, the road goes up a steep ridge, then drops back down again to run beside the marsh. All along this ridge is a fence that marks the refuge's boundary.

My son, Jeff, was with me and we were hurrying to reach Frenchglen, fifty some miles on down the road. As we sped past, I saw the pigeon. I was dumbstruck. So was Jeff when I slammed on the brakes. I turned the van around, came back, and the pigeon hadn't moved. I was able to get close and photograph it. Then it took flight and disappeared into the vastness. In 1990, when I learned that Carroll D. Littlefield was working on a book entitled *Birds of Malheur National Wildlife Refuge, Oregon*, I sent him a few transparencies of the bandtail. My wish was to get credit for this rare sighting, perhaps even my name in his book. He contacted me, and we discussed exactly where I had seen the pigeon. When he learned that the bird wasn't on the refuge side of the fence when I photographed it, he informed me that it didn't count. I countered by saying that we were talking about only a matter of yards, and when the pigeon flew it was heading in the direction of the refuge. But Littlefield was a tough referee, and his call stood.

In Baja there is a pale race of bandtail that has been called the Viosca's pigeon and is nonmigratory. In Central America the band-tailed pigeon is generally thought to range into Nicaragua. From Costa Rica south to Argentina and Peru, there is a white-naped pigeon, considered by most a bandtail, the sole difference being a gray underpart instead of white and a solid yellow bill, without the ink black tip present on a bandtail.

Away from the West Coast there is an important group of bandtails, *Patagioenas fasciata fasciata*, which is treated as a different race than the far western band-tailed pigeon, *Patagioenas fasciata monilis*. The northernmost breeding range of this eastern bandtail is in southwestern Colorado, into southern Utah, then southward into the eastern portion of Arizona, much of the mountainous region of New Mexico, a narrow band of West Texas, and down into central Mexico.

The population of this eastern race has remained stable over the years. Only the pigeons in Colorado have been subject to rises and falls. For example, estimates in 1942 showed 12,000 pigeons, while in 1952 the number was only 2221. Most years, however, it is thought to be around 5000 birds. Arizona's bandtails generally number around 100,000 birds, with New Mexico's population being about the same. Utah's figures are fragmented and because it lies on the extreme of the pigeon's interior range, the numbers can be expected to be lower than any state inhabited by this eastern race.

The Pacific race of bandtail, *Patagioenas fasciata monilis*, has a much larger population than the interior *fasciata*, although accurate estimates aren't available. I've never had an encounter with the interior race of bandtail in the United States. I have looked hard while in both Arizona and New Mexico hoping to see one.

Based on my profound interest in the pigeon, I am certain that the sight of a flock over pinon pines would be memorable. Yet I'll admit that the birds would seem out of place. For me, the band-tail is a bird of the wet rainy Pacific, the damp moss-covered Douglas firs, the deep alder-choked canyons, the fog off the cold ocean. To me, the band-tailed pigeon is a bird of the Northwest. Frankly, it seems out of place anywhere else. But then, I've also become moss covered due to exposure to nearly fifty years of Pacific winter storms.

Wings over the Firs

In passage down a mountain side, the flight is inconceivably swift, the wings being held close in to the sides, beating only at long intervals, and the body veering slightly from side to side in its arrow-like course. This headlong flight produces a rushing noise as of escaping steam.

GRINNELL, BRYANT, AND STORER 1918

TALK ABOUT timing—Meriwether Lewis and William Clark missed by a few short weeks, or perhaps days, being the first to record the band-tailed pigeon for science. If they had, this species would have been another new western bird for the expedition. Lewis and Clark had already encountered and described the greater sage-grouse, *Centrocerus urophasianus,* and the Columbian sharp-tailed grouse, *Tympanuchus phasianellus columbianus.* Their party reached the confluence of the Willamette River and the Columbia in Oregon during the first week of April 1806. This area annually supports many pairs of nesting bandtails. But early April was about a week too soon. Within the time frame when the pigeons would have been returning from the south in their spring migration, Lewis and Clark were well to the east, preparing to cross the Umatilla River.

It was fourteen years later that the first band-tailed pigeon was collected. During the summer of 1820 a bird from the race now known as *Patagioenas fasciata fasciata,* the interior bandtail, was collected by Colonel Stephen H. Long's expedition into the mountains near present-day Denver, Colorado. The specimen was later described to science by Thomas Say. The first pigeon of the Pacific race, *Patagioenas fasciata monilis,* was collected in Oregon by the early English botanist David Douglas. He shot the bird in August 1825 near the confluence of the Santiam and Willamette Rivers, which is just up the Willamette from the present-day ferry landing at Buena Vista. A few years later John James Audubon procured specimens of the pigeon from John Kirk Townsend, who collected in the Oregon Territory in 1836. Audubon wrote of the pigeon in *The Birds of America* (1827–1838):

> Many specimens have recently been obtained by Mr. Townsend, from whom I have procured three pairs of adult and some young birds. In my plate are represented two adult birds, placed on the branch of a superb species of dogwood, discovered by my learned friend Thomas Nuttall, Esq., when on his march toward the shores of the Pacific ocean, and which I have graced with his name! Mr. Townsend's notice respecting the bird here spoken of is as follows:
>
> "The Band-tailed pigeon is called by the Chinook Indians 'akoigh homin.' It ranges from the eastern spurs of the Rocky Mountains across to the Columbia River, where it is abundant. It arrived in 1836 in very great numbers, on the 17th of April, and continued in large flocks while breeding" . . .
>
> Mr. Nuttall has favoured me with an equally interesting notice: "This large and fine pigeon, always moving about in flocks, keeps in Oregon only in the thick forest of the Columbia and the Wahlamet, and during the summer is more particularly abundant in the alluvial groves of the

latter river, where throughout that season we constantly heard their cooing, or witnessed the swarming flocks feeding on the berries of the elder tree, those of the Great Cornel (*Cornus Nuttalli*), or before the ripening of berries, on the seed-germs or the young pods of the balsam poplar. They remain on the lower part of the Columbia nearly the whole year, late in the season (October and November) feeding mostly on the berries of the tree Cornel, but still they seem to migrate some distance to the south, as the severity of winter approaches."

The band-tailed pigeon is now the largest member of the order Columbiformes encountered in numbers within the continental United States. The coastal race of bandtails, *Patagioenas fasciata monilis,* is both darker in plumage and a few ounces heavier than the interior race, *P. fasciata fasciata.* In New Mexico, weights from the interior race range from 8.5 to 15.5 ounces; average weight for adult bandtails in Colorado is 11.2 ounces and juveniles weigh 9.5 ounces.

Inca dove (*Columbina inca*)

The order Columbiformes consists of pigeons, doves, and the extinct flightless dodo and solitaire of Mauritius, Rodriguez, and Reunion. Pigeons and doves, the Columbidae (a family within Columbiformes), comprise some 285 species worldwide.

Ornithologically, there is no distinction between a pigeon and a dove. The word *pigeon* is Norman-French and *dove* is Anglo-Saxon in origin. Over the years, however, the two words have come to differentiate size within the Columbidae. A large species is a pigeon while a small one is a dove, and the range in size varies greatly. For instance, the tiny diamond dove of Australia has the body size of the smallest of North American passerines. Its long, slender tail is almost comical when compared with its body. The largest, the jungle-dwelling crowned pigeon of New Guinea, is almost as large as a good-sized hen turkey.

Pigeons are found nearly worldwide, from the high Tibetan mountains to the forest floor of the wet, steaming tropics. More than half live within the geographical range of Indo-Malaya and Australia and are among some of the most lavishly colored representatives of the avian world. The plumage of pigeons ranges from the deepest of rich greens to reds, yellows, and blues. Some species certainly rival any of the vividly colored parrots.

red-billed pigeon (*Patagioenas flavirostris*)

The Columbiformes are set apart from other birds by their method of drinking. Pigeons and doves are able to take water without lifting their heads, while all others first take the water, then lift their heads to swallow. In addition, members of the family Columbidae possess another quite remarkable distinction: they produce a secretion commonly called *pigeon milk*. This thick, cheeselike substance is formed by epithelial cells in two dorsiventral portions of the bird's crop. The nutritious secretion is regurgitated for the young.

Worldwide, seven species of Columbidae have gone extinct, with most having vanished many years ago. These include the Bourbon pigeon in 1669, the Tanna ground-dove in 1774, and the Mauritius blue pigeon in 1830. Somewhat closer to the present, 1904, the Choiseul pigeon was added to the list. But a date much better known to many is September 1, 1914. It was on that day that a female passenger pigeon named Martha, the last of a small flock kept for many years by Prof. C. O. Whitman, was found dead in her cage at the Cincinnati Zoological Gardens.

A. W. Schorger, in his book, *The Passenger Pigeon: Its Natural History and Extinction* (1973), gave us this insight into Martha:

> It would be difficult to find a more garbled history than that of Martha. The more that was written about her, the worse the confusion. The following dates and times of death in 1914 occur in literature: 2:00 p.m., August 29, 1914; 2:00 p.m., September 1; 1:00 a.m., September 1; 1:00 p.m., September 1. That she died at 5:00 p.m. "surrounded by a hushed group of distinguished ornithologists" is sheer romance. The latest direct information derived from S. A. Stephan is that her lifeless body was found on the ground on September 1 at 1:00 p.m.
>
> This pigeon was promised to the Smithsonian Institu-

tion when she died. The body was suspended in water and the whole frozen. Encased in a 300 pound cake of ice, she arrived in Washington, D.C., September 4, 1914, where a detailed anatomical examination of the body was made by Shufeldt.

Unlike the band-tailed pigeon, there are many early writings and accounts regarding numbers of passenger pigeons. Often the numbers in these accounts make one pause in near disbelief. For example, in 1832 Alexander Wilson watched a flight of northward-bound passenger pigeons near Frankfort, Kentucky. He estimated the pigeons to number 2,230,272,000—two billion, two hundred and thirty million, two hundred and seventy-two thousand birds. And today this number is felt to be conservative based on his method of estimation!

Audubon also wrote of the awesome flocks of this era. A much quoted account came from his travels along the Ohio River in 1813: "The air was literally filled with pigeons; the light of noonday was obscured as by an eclipse, the dung fell in spots not unlike melting flakes of snow, and the continued buzz of wings had a tendency to lull my senses to repose."

The last great passenger pigeon nesting took place near Petoskey, Michigan, in 1877, and a much-reduced nesting took place near Grand Traverse, Michigan, in 1881. The Petoskey nesting site was documented by two naturalists, William Brewster and Jonathan Dwight, to extend northwest for twenty-eight miles and at its widest to be four miles across. Within this site any tree of size was reported to contain a nest, many with multiples. As staggering as the proportions of this site may appear, it is dwarfed by an earlier site in Wisconsin that was seventy-five miles long and up to fifteen miles wide.

In April 1885 Brewster and Dwight searched the hardwood and pine forests of Michigan for nesting passenger pigeons. They found one nest. With a speed that is difficult to grasp, the species had entered an era when, curiously enough, it would assume the same status as a fossilized coral that shares the name of the pigeon's last great nesting site—Petoskey.

IN THE HAWTHORN HEDGE

mourning dove (*Zenaida macroura*)

With the extinction of the passenger pigeon, the following members of the Columbidae now live in the United States and Canada.

COMMON AND SCIENTIFIC NAMES	PRESENT RANGE	STATUS
Band-tailed pigeon *Patagioenas fasciata*	From British Columbia southward into South America; also found in Colorado, Utah, Nevada, Arizona, New Mexico, Texas	Greatly reduced since 1900
Blue-headed quail-dove *Starnoenas cyanocephala*	Cuba, perhaps north into Florida Keys	Unknown
Common ground-dove *Columbina passerina*	Southern and southwestern United States into Mexico, Central and South America	Stable population
Inca dove *Columbina inca*	Southwestern United States into Mexico	Stable population
Key West quail-dove *Geotrygon chrysia*	Caribbean Islands, north into the Florida Keys	Reduced numbers
Mourning dove *Zenaida macroura*	Nearly all of the United States, southern Canada, and a wide range in Mexico	Numerous in some regions, greatly reduced in some former ranges
Red-billed pigeon *Patagioenas flavirostris*	Most of Mexico into Central and South America; northernmost limit is southern Texas	Stable population

COMMON AND SCIENTIFIC NAMES	PRESENT RANGE	STATUS
Ringed turtle-dove[†] *Streptopelia risoria*	Southern California, Florida, Texas	Stable and increasing population
Rock dove, common or park pigeon[†] *Columba livia*	Southern Canada, entire United States, Mexico, and Central America	Abundant population
Spotted dove[†] *Streptopelia chinensis*	Hawaiian Islands, southern California	Stable population
White-crowned pigeon *Patagioenas leucocephala*	Most of the Caribbean region, including Central America and northern South America; northernmost range includes the Florida Keys and the Everglades	Greatly reduced in numbers
White-tipped dove *Leptotila verreauxi*	Mexico, Central and South America, and north into a small area in extreme southern Texas	Stable population
White-winged dove *Zenaida asiatica*	Southwestern United States into Mexico	Greatly reduced population
Zebra dove[†] *Geopelia striata*	Hawaiian Islands	Stable population
Zenaida dove *Zenaida aurita*	Caribbean Islands, north into the Florida Keys	Stable population

[†]Species introduced to the United States and Canada from their native ranges.

white-crowned pigeon (*Patagioenas leucocephala*)

Having stated that the bandtail is a bird which has firmly held my interest for over fifty years, I will have to admit that of all the North American pigeons and doves, I think the white-crowned pigeon (*Patagioenas leucocephala*) has the most striking plumage. But second, and not that far behind in my eye, is the band-tailed pigeon. Certainly the most complete description of the band-tail's plumage was given by Grinnell, Bryant, and Storer (1918). The following may be more detailed than most are interested in, but is offered for the record:

> Adults, both sexes. Head pinkish brown or vinaceous (exact tint varying greatly among different individuals), darkest and more purplish on top and back of head, more ashy on chin and cheeks; base of bill straw yellow, and black; naked eyelids, coral red; narrow collar around hind neck, white, averaging more conspicuous in males; broad area on sides and back of neck (below white collar), iridescent bronzy green; back, dark olive brown; rump and bases of tail feathers, dark bluish gray; ill-defined band across middle tail, dull black; terminal portions of tail feathers, drab, coverts narrowly margined with white, flight feathers, brownish black; lining of wing and axillars, gray; under surface of flight feathers, dull brown; under surface of body, pinkish brown or vinaceous, deepest on breast and sides, paling to almost white on belly; under tail coverts, white; under surface of terminal portion of tail, whitish, distinctly lighter than upper surface of same; feet straw yellow. In some females the tone of coloration verges toward grayish rather than pinkish brown. Juvenile plumage: Similar to that of adult, but vinaceous tinge wholly lacking; neck without white collar or iridescent bronzing; under surface dark brownish, with feather tippings of lighter color, giving a faintly scaled effect.

band-tailed pigeon (*Patagioenas fasciata*)

You will note that the band in band-tailed pigeon is described as being an "ill-defined band across middle tail, dull black." That is somewhat misleading. Admittedly, the band isn't evident most of the time—it only shows when the pigeon spreads its tail to act as a brake when settling into a tree, or when the male performs his breeding flight. But in either case, though the band across the tail is a dull black, it shows up strikingly and can be seen from some distance. Overall, in my opinion, an adult male bandtail on an emerald green Douglas fir bough is about as beautiful a bird as the Northwest has to offer.

The Single Egg

If you follow the pigeons to their breeding grounds in some remote canyon you will be struck by the owl-like hooting that fills the place, and you will locate the sound here and there along the sides of the canyon at dead tree tops, in each of which a solitary male is sunning himself, at intervals puffing out his breast and hooting.

FLORENCE BAILEY 1902

AFTER WORLD WAR II, youngsters in Oregon's Willamette Valley had the best of the valley's rich agricultural base for nearly twenty-five years. Especially in the 1950s, nearly every child joined a berry-and-bean platoon during the summer months. The goal was simple: earn as much money as possible to buy school clothes for the coming year. Parents were largely free from this financial burden as a result. Pendleton woolens—shirts for boys, skirts for girls—were especially sought after. There was unmistakable status associated with having a large collection of Pendletons. Of course, the harder one worked, the more Pendletons one could buy.

The platoons were based around strawberries and pole beans. Strawberries were picked in June, and beans started in late July, lasting until State Fair week in late August. During the spare time between these two major crops, cherries could be picked. All the children who picked these crops were under the age of sixteen. Once reaching sixteen, we spent the summer in one of the many fruit and vegetable canneries once found in the Willamette Valley. More money was earned in the canneries than by picking, so aside from buying clothes, many first cars were made possible by summer's end. All of this came to a halt during the mid-1970s, when labor laws made it impossible for those under sixteen to work in the fields and many farmers switched to other crops. But at the height of the era, the berry-and-bean platoons were truly a wonderful way to spend the summer.

The platoons were often formed by schoolteachers or mothers seeking summer employment. The farmers rented the buses, and the platoon leaders drove them and then straw-bossed the kids in the fields. To catch the bus I woke at five o'clock to eat breakfast, packed my lunch, then hurried out of the house into the morning to wait to be picked up. Regarding lunch, the all-important trick to keep my can of pop cool was to freeze it, then wrap it in foil before catching the bus. By lunch it would be thawed, but still icy cold. In Oregon in June during the strawberry harvest, even if the temperature soared into the high eighties in the afternoons, the mornings were noticeably cool, even cold. I would stand waiting for the bus, clad in a sweatshirt that would later be removed, and frequently would shiver before the bus arrived. Of course, in the Northwest people sleep under a blanket most nights, and air conditioners are something few people have, or if they do, seldom use.

In 1956, my first year of platoon picking, the bus picked me up directly in front of our house. At that time, before the neighborhood dissolved into a residential sprawl, there was a ten-acre fir forest across the street from our front yard. On one of those cool early mornings during my first year, I came out of the house to be met by the loud hooting of a band-tailed pigeon somewhere deep in the firs.

The sound, in the otherwise still morning, stopped me abruptly. Until that moment I had never heard a bandtail, and as a newcomer to the West from Virginia, I had seen only a few. But the sound coming from the shroud of fir limbs was not one made by an owl, of that much I was certain. In the span of time it took me to look excitedly for the source, the pigeon left the dead snag on which it had been perched.

Its flight was a steady, spiraling climb, one made of various changes in directions, but appeared to have little, if any, urgency associated with it. When the bird reached a height above the tallest of the firs, it stopped its upward progress and, for all practical purposes, froze. The tail was spread to its full width, the wings locked for an instant, transforming the gray bird into a shadow against the rich blue sky.

In a moment, the pigeon dropped a few feet straight down and began flapping its wings hard, kestrel-like, to remain stationary at a set height. Then it locked its wings again, making a few lazy circles, dropping lower to repeat the act. In two minutes it was down on the snag again, and the hooting resumed. On three consecutive mornings I was able to witness this spellbinding display, begrudgingly forced to leave after watching far too short a time due to the screeching arrival of the bean bus.

The bandtail's call is most often likened to that of an owl's, rather than the normal rolling *coo* of a pigeon. The call is very deep, filling the forest around the calling bird. It is a call that, once heard and known, will not be mistaken. For his master's work at Oregon State University (1970), Daniel Keppie recorded bandtail calls as a part of an audio index technique he developed. He noted that bandtail males call over a range of one to twelve audible notes per call, with the four- and five-note calls used most frequently.

NOTES PER CALL	NUMBER OF CALLS RECORDED
1	5
2	18
3	48
4	173
5	134
6	91
7	61
8	28
9	14
10	4
11	6
12	2

A male bandtail will come forth with the call at any time, sometimes without a clear purpose, over much of the year. But generally the call is associated with the advent of breeding season, which can begin as early as March in the pigeon's most southern range and usually July in the northern range. Yet I once heard the call from within a flock of very late migrating Oregon bandtails huddled in a low fir swaying against a strong November wind.

But at no time is the call more apparent—certainly more pronounced—than during the early mornings of late June, most of July, and early August. Most of the calling commences after the sun has risen, but I've heard the calls a few times at very first light, before the normal movements and sounds of the forest are expected to be heard. These early calls were likely a reflex of the pigeon as it first stirred to meet a new day.

While the male will continue his call throughout the summer into the early fall with a lesser degree of regularity than at the onset of the breeding season, the male's nuptial flight seems to be reserved for a short period of days prior to copulation.

On the Pacific Coast the band-tailed pigeon's nesting activity corresponds almost directly to the latitude in which the bird is found. The extremes include the early date of March 5 in southern California, to a very late, rare October 17 nesting near Seattle, Washington. Past records for Oregon and Washington point strongly to May and June as the prime nesting season for the band-tailed pigeon, with British Columbia's breeding season comparable to these months. But even with the wealth of information compiled on the bandtail during the past two decades, a specific nesting period is difficult to speak of with any degree of authority. It is now known, however, that May nestings are not common, as they once were thought to be.

In Colorado the nesting activity of the interior race of band-tailed pigeon seems to closely correspond with that of the Pacific race. In that state nesting has been recorded primarily in late July through August. However, in the southern range of Arizona, New Mexico, and Mexico, late April and the entire month of May appear to be the prime months.

Oddly, one of the first scientific reports on the band-tailed pigeon's habits attributed two characteristics of the pigeon's nesting that seldom occur: the laying of two eggs and ground nesting. John Kirk Townsend, traveling along the Columbia River in 1836, collected specimens of the bandtail for his friend John James Audubon. On April 17 of that year he noted that the band-tailed pigeon was an abundant bird along the river. He also stated that the pigeon's breeding grounds were on the banks of the river, on the ground without a nest, and two eggs were laid. How Townsend came up with this information is a mystery.

But even more remarkable was Dr. Albert Gregory Prill's 1893 insight into bandtail nesting. Dr. Prill was a physician from Scio, Oregon. Aside from his practice, he was deeply engaged in ornithology. Prill amassed a large collection of bird skins and eggs, as well as published notes in a wide range of journals and magazines based on his fieldwork. He was credited with collecting several new species in Oregon, and his skins and eggs were deposited in the U.S. National Museum in Washington, D.C., the California Academy of Sciences, and the University of Oregon. His local fame was such that a pristine lake in Oregon's Cascade Mountains was named Prill Lake.

Writing in the *Oologist* in 1893, Prill also stated that the bandtail laid two eggs. Then he continued with a belief that is best addressed with a "What?": he wrote that bandtails took their eggs with them during daily flights. Prill believed that they did the incubating in stages, in different trees, as the mood struck them. Fifteen years later, articles still appeared in ornithological journals causing him grief over his statement. I have often wondered how he ever lived that down.

A few, and likely very few, bandtails do lay two eggs. To date no one has attempted to attach a percentage to the number of bandtail pairs with two eggs. As for ground nesting, there have been scattered records, all treated as a novelty. And generally these nests were not on the ground, rather on the high cut stumps of trees. During the early logging of the Northwest, stumps were commonly left that were from three to six feet in height.

Nesting of bandtail pairs in close proximity has been documented. But unlike passenger pigeons, more than one pair per tree is nearly unheard of. The lone and unique case of a tree containing more than one pair was reported by H. Garvin Smith in 1934 from New Mexico. He found 17 nests in a single Douglas fir. However, one wonders if most of these were nests from previous years.

Although there have been many observations of certain areas in the Northwest containing multiple pairs of nesting bandtails, it was felt that the breeding population of pigeons was well distributed over a wide region. Early writings formed the concept of a single pair with miles of forest between it and the next pair. Later studies lowered the estimate of the area used: figures of two to four acres per pair or territories of one-tenth to one-half mile radius are now accepted.

Based on studies done at mineral sites, it appears that loose colonies are far more common than thought in the past. These colonies are located in the immediate vicinity of mineral springs or tidal flats, which the Pacific race uses on a daily basis during breeding. This insight has become very important in the total understanding of the band-tailed pigeon.

A Thin Platform of Sticks

The combination of flimsily constructed nests and high winds is responsible for considerable losses of eggs and young birds.

MACGREGOR AND SMITH 1955

WES BATTERSON became a folk hero on the northern Oregon coast. A very small man, Wes came from old pioneer stock: his grandfather, William Batterson, settled on the South Fork of the Nehalem River in 1877, and his father, Samuel Batterson, raised cattle and operated the Nehalem Valley Meat Company. Wes was born on September 30, 1909, on the family homestead. A small settlement—today represented by only a few homes—was once a town named Batterson. Wes's fame was based on his work with wildlife. As a small boy he had a special "something" in his dealings and knowledge with animals and birds. Over his lifetime one frequently heard of Wes's special gift. I have been told he could whistle birds to his outstretched hand.

Those outside of the hamlet of Nehalem, where Wes settled as a young man, first had contact with him in the mid-1930s. William L. Finley, the famed Oregon wildlife photographer, heard of Wes and paid him a visit. Finley was dumbstruck to find that Wes was very successful in raising both blue and ruffed grouse (*Dendragapus obscurus* and *Bonasa umbellus*). These two birds are wilderness species, and for all practical purposes they are nearly impossible to keep in captivity. To breed them was unheard of, yet Wes did it on a yearly basis.

43

To do this, he constructed aviaries deep in the timber and brush of Oregon's Coast Range, then he fed the birds and their broods with all natural foods. This amounted to an incredible amount of effort, as the chief food source he used was grubs he gathered from tearing up downed logs. During the berry season, he supplemented the insects with fruit.

Largely due to Finley's reports about this amazing talent, Wes's name spread. Members of the old Oregon Game Commission began to contact him regularly about various wildlife matters along the northern Oregon coast. In the early 1940s, Wes was hired as a game biologist, even though he had only a high school education.

Some of his first job assignments included being sent into the vast sagebrush regions of eastern Oregon to study sage-grouse. Wes and his wife lived in a small trailer for nearly a year in the grouse's habitat. He told me once that he and his wife certainly got to know each other well during the period, as they rarely saw anyone else.

As the years passed, Wes Batterson became somewhat of a legend. For example, the U.S. Fish and Wildlife Service secured the loan of Wes from Oregon. He was sent to Hawaii to work with the few remaining Nene geese. In Oregon, his seasonal counts of game birds were always far greater than those by any other biologist in the state. It wasn't because Wes had more birds in the territory he counted. While other biologists drove roads for their counts, Wes went into the brush on foot for his counts and frequently used his whistles and voice calls to make the birds show themselves.

I met Wes in the early 1960s, and in 1974 I turned to him for help with some bandtail projects. At the time, Wes very likely had the longest continual contact with the pigeons of anyone. He had moved the short distance from Batterson to Nehalem after marrying and had built a small house on several acres. Here he kept a wide assortment of waterfowl and game birds, including band-tailed pigeons. But more importantly, he attracted a very large flock of wild bandtails into his back yard each spring and summer. He fed the pigeons daily with wheat and cracked corn on feeding platforms. His location was ideal. Wes's home was at the base of Neahkahnie Mountain, about a half mile from Nehalem Bay. He was in a direct flight line from the breeding habitat of the mountain to the estuary, where the breeding pigeons went each day to drink.

During the first research project on the band-tailed pigeon carried out by Oregon State University, Wes's huge flock of daily visiting pigeons was studied. Wes constructed a trap, triggered from a release near his back door. Over several years he banded more pigeons than anyone previously had done. In fact, Wes's banding, in terms of numbers of birds, has never been equaled since. Also during his long association with the pigeon, he made a 16-mm movie of the life history of the bandtail.

During a period when I was seeking a pigeon's nest to photograph, I visited Wes. We spent a morning on the side of Neahkahnie Mountain. Wes is a small man, and to watch him scurry through the timber was a study in motion. He did so with the speed of a pine squirrel. All the time he kept up a wide assortment of bird whistles to the passerines we encountered. I didn't see him call one down to his hand, but he most certainly had them perch directly over his head. In rather short order he found a band-tailed pigeon nest. It was a new nest, without an egg. But the following week, the second week in July, when I revisited the site a single pure white egg was present. I got my photographs.

Although there are reports to the contrary, nest building prior to laying of the egg in bandtails closely follows the pattern of the rock dove. The male is the one that builds the nest. Only once have I been so fortunate as to be able to witness this. And during breakfast no less!

In August 1957 a male bandtail began a nest thirty feet up in a Douglas fir in the backyard of my parents' house in Salem, Oregon. The bird was in plain sight from the vantage point of our breakfast table. Over the course of four mornings, and once during the late afternoon, the pigeon appeared with small sticks to construct the nest.

The majority of materials were brought in from elsewhere. The male then sat for as long as a half hour before walking or flap-flying to the selected location near the base of two closely spaced limbs. On a couple of occasions the bird dropped the stick he had arrived with. He then showed no interest in the loss for a long period, and no attempt was made to fly down to reclaim it. Instead he left and returned with another. Only once did he secure a stick from the tree itself, breaking off a dead stick from a branch above him. Nor did he seem very interested in completing the project. During the four mornings he only managed to place about ten sticks, then ceased activity and abandoned the work. At no time did the female appear.

Even with just ten or so sticks in place, the nest was nearly done. Almost all bandtail nests are little more than a makeshift platform of sticks. Unlike rock doves, the bandtail doesn't seem to work the materials into any sort of solid structure. Viewed from the bottom, the bandtail's nest often shows gaps with light filtering through. Being little more than a pile, and not a very large pile, it is somewhat of a wonder that such structures support the weight of brooding adults and survive the growth of the squab, which becomes very active during the last few days of its nest occupancy. Old bandtail nests frequently appear to be nothing more than the natural accumulations of fallen sticks caught in the forks of branches over the passage of time.

Placement of the nest, along with the favored nesting sites, varies depending on the geographical region. In the Huachuca Mountains of Arizona, live oaks are favored. In Colorado, lodgepole pine are used, and in California, various oaks. In British Columbia, Washington, and Oregon band-tailed pigeons prefer to nest in conifers.

Reports list the height of the nest from 10 to 180 feet off the ground. In locales directly affected by strong marine winds off the Pacific, the nests can be found considerably lower. Of the scores of old nests that Wes Batterson and I checked on Neahkahnie Mountain, a large percentage were no higher than seven feet from the ground. However, all were built within the sheltered confines of exceedingly dense conifers. The active nest we

managed to locate was placed in the fork of a sturdy fir bough, four feet from the forest floor.

A bandtail egg is pure white, glossy, and about the size of a racing homer pigeon or rock dove's, which is about half the size of a small chicken egg. In the thin stick nest, the egg is a stark example of the jeopardy of living in nature. As with domestic pigeons, bandtails time the completion of the nest to correspond with the laying of the egg (or eggs). Incubation starts almost as soon as the egg is laid.

The incubation period can range from fifteen to eighteen days. Upon hatching, the squab is totally helpless, is scantily covered with a very thin yellow fuzz, and appears weak to the point that it has little power of neck and head coordination. Within a week, the squab is uniformly covered in its prefeather fuzz, has gained some power of movement, and has become vocal with a small squeal that precedes feeding or signals the wish to be fed if the adults are near.

All pigeons and doves feed their young with a secretion known as pigeon milk. Johnson A. Neff, in his 1947 *Habits, Food, and Economic Status of the Band-tailed Pigeon*, provided the best documentation of this unusual feeding method:

> Little is known of the development of this secretion in the band-tailed pigeon. Even in regard to the domestic pigeon the literature lacks information on some phases that are of interest, but since the domestic pigeon incubates for 18 days and the young remain in the nest for at least 30 days, it seems probable that the development of the pigeon milk and the duration of the supply may be similar in the two species. . . .
>
> About the 8th day of incubation the lobes of the pigeon's crop begin to increase in size through multiplication of the

cells of the outer, or proliferating layer; by the 12th day the walls of the lobes are obviously thickened and enlarged and on the 18th day they are at their greatest development. The inner layer of each lobe has been pushed farther away from the source of blood in the outer layer, and it begins to degenerate; globules of fat develop in the cells, and whitish masses of dead cells begin to peel off. By the time the eggs hatch on the 18th day these greasy masses are sufficient to furnish the entire food of the squabs during their first few days of life. After the first few days the regurgitated material begins to contain some quantity of seeds and other solids that have been softened in the crop of the adults. It is said that the duration of the milk supply varies considerably in the different families of the domestic pigeon, and that in some it has ceased to form by the time the young are 7 days old, whereas in others approximately half of the food is still "milk" when the young have reached 10 days of age.

Neff also provided an account of the growth of the squab, based on almost daily tabulation of events in two bandtail nests in Colorado in August 1945:

At one day of age the squab was a tiny helpless creature about 2 inches long. The female parent was on the nest when it was found at 2 p.m. on August 22, and she remained on the nest during the daylight hours of August 24. The male was on the nest during most of the day of August 23. During the remainder of the study the adults followed this routine: The male returned to the nest between 8:45 and 9:30 a.m. each day and brooded the young bird during the day. The female returned to the nest at any time between 3:45 and 5:15 p.m. She was not observed feeding the youngster, though she undoubtedly must have fed it. Watched from dawn until dark, the tiny squab appeared to sleep until after the return of the male. During the first week about three feedings, all between noon and 3 p.m., seemed to be the schedule. As the youngster's food capacity grew, the number of feedings was reduced to two, and the period of regurgitation indicated that a large quantity of food was taken. Both feedings were about midday.

The adults continued to hover the squab, both day and night, until it was 20 days old. On that date they stopped abruptly and did not return to the nest during either day or night except to feed the squab. Each parent came to the nest once daily, between 10 and 11 a.m., fed the squab, and departed. Occasionally during the day one of the parents would visit the vicinity, scan the nest and its surroundings carefully, and then depart.

During the first 10 days the young squab did not grow very rapidly. It slept most of the day and increased in size, but the feather development seemed to be slow. After about 12 days feather development began visibly to progress. At 17 days of age one of the squabs was well covered with feathers, the body feathers being about 15 mm out of the sheath and the first primary 30 mm out of the sheath; the tail feathers measured 28 mm from the tip of the tail flesh to the tip of the feathers; the head was heavily pin feathered but had no open feathers, and the sides were quite bare. The yellowish brown down adhered to the tips of the feathers, giving the squab a peculiar fuzzy appearance. At this age the youngster crawled clumsily about over the nest and snapped its beak furiously at the intruder. It weighed 140 grams, or 4.9 ounces. External examination indicated that the crop was well filled with pigeon milk.

When the squab was 23 days of age its outward appearance had changed little, but when the writer's hand approached, the young bird snapped its beak vigorously, struck with bent wing, and danced awkwardly about over the nest. When the squab was 26 days old it weighed 243 grams and its tail measured 75 mm. For the first time it spent much time preening, apparently picking off the down that still adhered to the tips of the feathers. On that day also, one of the squabs began to exercise and spent much of the day walking about, for the first time venturing off the nest onto the nest branch, waving and flapping its wings, and craning and peering about with interest. This was repeated on the 27th day, and on the 30th day the bird was gone from the nest, tree, and immediate area. The other squab was not observed between its 20th and 26th day, but on the latter day it was sitting quietly on the nest without apparent interest in exercising. The nest was not again visited.

Once the squab has become fully fledged, it is on its own. In all likelihood the adult birds stop their visits to the nest area a few days prior to the juvenile's leaving. As previously stated, large flocks of bandtails are commonly encountered during April, May, and early June, prior to nesting activity. According to my observations, there has always been a period when these flocks disperse, sometime between mid-June and early August. Then once again the flocks began to reappear. These reformed flocks are likely the grouping of late June and July juveniles combined with first-year breeding adults, which are thought to begin breeding at a later date than older second- or third-year pairs.

In my slide collection of bandtail photographs, I have a transparency of three pigeons in flight. The photograph was taken on September 16, 1975. It shows clearly an adult pair followed by a juvenile. I had given it little thought until Mike Passmore, a band-tail researcher at Oregon State University, became interested in it. He pointed out that it was obviously a family group and the juvenile had stayed with the adults after leaving the nest. After that, I made a point of watching for other family groups. In most cases it is difficult late in the season, as the pigeons have reformed in flocks, but on three other occasions I have seen family groups.

Among those involved with the mathematics of game bird management, it has always been understood that the bandtail has the lowest breeding output of any game bird in the United States. For many years it was considered fact that the band-tailed pigeon only raised one young per season. Today, however, we know that older pairs frequently nest twice a season. What isn't known is the success rate of these twice-nesting pairs or what percentage of the total pigeon population are old, twice-nesting birds. In the end, it all still amounts to the fact that the bandtail is critically slow to build upon its numbers. There have been some terrible consequences as a result.

Seasonal Smorgasbord

The antics of these birds were more like the acrobatic stunts of parrots than of pigeons. They would walk out on the slender branches till they tipped down, then, hanging by their feet, would secure an acorn and drop off to alight on a branch lower down.

F. C. WILLARD 1916

IN A HARDBOUND journal in which I record about everything I do in the outdoors, the entry for June 6, 1976, includes a sighting of band-tailed pigeons. Ken Durbin and I had hiked a couple of miles down through the rolling sand dunes to reach an estuary on the northern Oregon coast formed by the confluence of the Big and Little Nestucca Rivers. Here we planned to fly-fish for sea-run cutthroat trout.

The fishing in itself justified the emphasis that I placed on the day when I recorded it in the journal—that night upon our return, rather than letting it slide for a day or two, as I generally am in the habit of doing. For the sea-run cutthroat is akin to the bandtail in a multitude of ways. The trout is a species of the Northwest, not entirely understood, present, yet often unknown or unnoticed by the human inhabitants of its range. In salt water it is a rover, moving freely, and often without a trace of passage. In the past, when the band-tailed pigeon was little understood, it too was known as a rover.

In Washington and British Columbia, small numbers of fly

fishermen over the years have been exceedingly proficient in taking the cutthroat trout in salt water. In Oregon, however, this was largely or totally unheard of. It seems that the Oregon cutthroat spends its ocean phase far offshore, deep under the waves of the Pacific. In the last days of August and into September, the cutthroat enter the rivers for the spawning run, gaining the fish its once common name of "harvest trout." But since no one that Ken and I knew had ever really tried to fish for the sea-run cutthroats in Oregon's bays and estuaries, we were left with the haunting possibility that the trout might be there to a larger degree than known. If so, then we were on to something very good.

For me, both the band-tailed pigeon and the sea-run cutthroat enhance the strong regional flavor of the Northwest and in particular the landscape abutting the Pacific. They just seem to firmly belong. On that June morning as Ken and I waded the estuary, both using a Silver Brown, Roderick Haig-Brown's famed sea-run fly, we looked directly back at the Coast Range. From sea level the mountains appear much higher than they actually are, more bumps than mountains really: a blend of deep green firs and silver-gray alder.

Behind us were the dunes, sharply dipped in places, the low spots filled with winter rains to form clear freshwater ponds, the high points of the dunes covered with brown knee-high coarse grass, a mark of the past work of the Civilian Conservation Corps during the 1930s. A couple of hundred yards out into the dunes stood an odd, solitary, dense pine grove of about two acres, the trees squat and deformed by the winds off the Pacific and totally surrounded by sand and water.

We were fishing an incoming tide. Several thousand casts had resulted in nothing. It was exactly the same result as we had experienced in other Oregon saltwater areas we had tried. Ken was wading out further than me, casting, searching, exploring the shallow trenches that were beginning to form as the water rushed in. As the tide reached full high, he began casting back toward shore. He finally caught one, a very nice, bright silver, twelve-inch sea-run, and there was great excitement over that single fish.

But there were no more. In fact, that was the one and only sea-run either of us caught as the result of our research. After that day we didn't try again for sea-runs in salt water, even though there was some nagging feeling that the estuary down at Florence should be sampled. We walked back over the dunes about an hour after Ken had caught the trout, and in doing so we crossed close to the pine grove. As we passed, a pair of bandtails flew out. A few steps further, a score thundered out and away. In total, there were about fifty in the air as they left. I will never tire of seeing band-tails, and that day was no different. With some pigeons still in the pines, I put a 300-mm lens on the camera and crept from tree to tree trying to get the pigeons silhouetted against the sky.

Ken, I'm sure, was mildly amused by my burst of excitement. But bandtails do that to me. As I attempted to photograph the pigeons, I started to question just what they were doing there. They were in a single small wooded patch, with miles of sand, thousands of miles of ocean behind them, and the usual forest habitat of the Coast Range better than a mile in front.

My question was answered a few minutes later when we put up a small flock out of the groundcover. Salal. I looked for ber-ries, and of course at that time of year there were none, but each low waxy bush was in full flower. The pigeons were feeding on salal blossoms, one of their first foods upon returning to the coastal portions of the Northwest.

As for what else bandtails feed on, the reports have been some-what sketchy. The only laboratory study that I am aware of was carried out in the 1930s. This study was based on the examination of 639 bandtail crops and stomachs. The result was seventy-six separate classes of plant food, twenty-two of which were found at a frequency of at least 0.5 percent. When looking at the table, however, keep in mind that this study was based on the Pacific pigeons rather than the interior race. Much more importantly, the bandtails collected for the study came from California during the pigeon's wintering period, which can be as long as seven months. Therefore, acorns were the single most important foodstuff for the pigeon, comprising 43 percent of their winter diet.

FOOD ITEM	FREQUENCY OF OCCURRENCE (%)
Unidentified acorns	18.2
Cultivated cherries	12.4
Dogwood fruits	11.7
Live oak acorns	11.1
Wheat	10.3
Garden peas	7.4
Elderberry fruits	6.4
Madrona berries	6.1
Wild cherry fruits	6.0
Cultivated oats	5.8
Miscellaneous vegetable debris	4.4
Salal fruits	3.8
Manzanita seeds and flowers	3.1
Cultivated prunes	3.0
Cascara fruits	2.8
Interior live oak acorns	2.0
Pinon nuts	1.9
Emory oak acorns	1.7
California black oak acorns	1.6
Oak blossoms	1.3
Oregon white oak acorns	0.8
Yellow pine seeds	0.5

Source: U.S. Bureau of Biological Survey (1936)

In the forty-seven years since I first made contact with the band-tailed pigeon, I have only seen it feeding on acorns during two years, 1958 and 1963. Both of these occurrences were in Oregon and in late September. I am certain that there have been other years in my region when pigeons sought acorns, I just haven't seen them do so. In my experience, the bandtail has always been a berry bird. These berries, in the order they are used, are red elderberry, cascara, Pacific or western dogwood (*Cornus nuttallii*), and blue elderberry. In nearly all cases, once the blue elderberry is gone in late September, so are the bandtails.

During late August and into the first several weeks of September, cascara, Pacific dogwood, and blue elderberry can all have berries. Moreover, I know of several places where all three grow within close range of one another. Thus, the pigeons have a choice. But when they do, it is the cascara that wins, hands down. Band-tailed pigeons simply love the big, huckleberry-sized, deep purple berries. Also, and of some importance, bandtails appear to travel distances to feed on cascara berries.

The cascara tree is a Northwest legend in itself. Very few people called it *cascara*, though. Rather it was *chittim*, which was the polite term for *shittim*. The bark of the cascara was once used to make a very strong laxative. Today it still is used, but to a very small extent, as nearly all laxatives are now synthetics. Also cascara laxative was noted as being harsh in terms of relieving constipation. In fact, the Chinook Indian word for the tree was *wahoo*, a fact I have always found remarkably humorous.

Species of the genus *Rhamnus*, the buckthorns, are found on four continents. The species used for laxative are *Rhamnus catharticus* of Africa, Europe, and Siberia and our own *R. purshianus*. The North American cascara bark was first publicized by Dr. J. H. Bundy in 1877. As a result, major drug firms sought the bark, the foremost being those in London. By 1900 nearly 800

David Hagerbaumer

tons of dry bark from Oregon and Washington was exported to London each year.

All bark was peeled by hand in the summer, a slow and hot job. Like many Northwest youngsters, I peeled cascara bark, dried it on my parents' garage roof, and sold it to a cascara buyer in downtown Salem, Oregon. In the late 1950s I was paid fifteen cents a pound for the dried bark. The bark was still commonly peeled then, and there was a ready market for it, but the glory days of cascara had long passed.

The 1920s saw the height of the cascara bark frenzy. So much was peeled that thousands of wild trees were killed. This was the result of peeling a standing tree. If a peeler first cut the cascara down, leaving about three inches of stump, the tree would re-sprout. Apparently many peelers didn't bother to do this, how-ever. In the late 1920s Oregon State University became involved in several large cascara tree farms to try to take the pressure off wild cascara, but these were abandoned when the price for the bark declined during the grim years of the Depression.

While the bark of the cascara is all-powerful (the dust from dried bark can trigger results if inhaled), the berries contain none of the laxative element. And with this fact ends a famous and oft-repeated Northwest logging camp tale—of the newcomer who was served what he thought was huckleberry pie, made of cascara berries. The tale has several different endings as to the ef-fect resulting from eating most of the pie. However, the tales of peeling and then slipping cascara bark into the water barrels of roadside laborers or farm workers are based on true happenings.

Today, especially in the Coast Range from northern California into British Columbia, the cascara is a common tree. In some locales it grows in groves. Most mature cascara trees are about fifteen feet high and ten inches in diameter, with a few being larger. One very old tree reportedly found during the 1920s in

Washington was a remarkable sixty feet in height and three feet in diameter. That would have been a large cascara indeed.

Cascaras are most often encountered near creeks or rivers. They require open, sunlit areas. Faster growing alders and Douglas firs will often outgrow cascaras, block out the sunlight, and eventually kill them. Cascaras do best in the years after a wild fire or after hillsides have been logged off.

When the bandtails return from their wintering grounds in California to the Northwest in April, there are no berries to feed on. During the first month or so, blossoms and pollen make up much of their diet. But they are also quick to take advantage of waste grain from spring plantings. Most commonly this is witnessed in farm fields, but I once watched, with considerable amazement, a very large gathering of bandtails intermingled with feral rock doves feeding along the railroad tracks in the aged concrete and brick confines of Portland, Oregon. Bandtails feeding in spring-planted fields have been described as a "long blue ribbon sweeping across the brown earth." It is a very apt image.

In the 1930s there were outcries from farmers in the Puget Sound region of Washington that bandtails were eating great amounts of sowed seeds, principally peas. This proved to be unfounded, as the pigeons only pick up what is lying loose and do not scratch the earth to uncover seeds as other birds commonly do. During the 1960s, Oregon State University pigeon researchers cannon-netted bandtails in fields during the early spring. The researchers were undertaking a banding program, and they found the best results were in fields very near the foothills, rather than out in the valley floor.

During the early 1970s there was a particularly heavy run of summer steelhead in an Oregon coastal river. I was late one morning and driving fast to reach the river. Rounding a series of sharp S-turns into the foothills of the Coast Range, I passed a plot of ground that was black with Brewer's blackbirds and the much larger gray-blue forms of bandtails. I slowed down as I passed and saw more pigeons coming from the timber. I drove on, thinking about what I had seen, thinking about the need to get on the water before the first strong sunlight hit several of my favorite runs. After a debate of ten minutes or so, I turned the car around and went back. I was glad I did.

I crawled along a brushy fence out to where the pigeons were feeding. The field had been sowed to oats. The birds showed little fear as they worked the ground searching for loose grain. I spent better than three hours watching the pigeons, sitting with my back comfortably against a fence post. The entire flock would group, then move forward in a long line, the pigeons in the rear flying up to advance to the head. It was a hurried march, with the birds almost running. Spasmodically, the entire flock would burst into the air and fly rapidly to tall firs bordering the field. Then they would glide back down after a brief period.

By May some of the berries and fruits begin to form, and bandtails feed on them in the green state to a heavy extent. At one time I had a house bordered by an old cherry orchard with about a dozen trees. In the mornings the bandtails would flock into the orchard. I could stand in my front yard and watch them pass. They were after the very small, green cherries. As the fruit became larger, they fed on it less. When it was fully ripe, no pigeons came.

Given the chance, and with foodstuffs they like, bandtails can eat a remarkable amount at one time. Johnson Neff recorded the highest single-crop counts for individual bandtails feeding on various foods: 26 whole cultivated cherries, 227 whole garden peas, 22 whole California live oak acorns, 56 whole Emory oak acorns, 725 whole kernels of wheat, 660 kernels of oats, and 104 cascara berries. There is a report of a bandtail in southern Oregon eating green prunes in such numbers it couldn't fly. And there are other reports of bandtails feeding on acorns to the extent that the sharp points present in the nuts of some species pierced the crop wall and protruded out, causing the leakage of crop fluids and staining the breast feathers.

In the Northwest bandtails feed largely on the red elderberry during June and July. In some areas, especially if there is a heavy growth of red elderberries, the feeding can be done in flocks. But in most cases the pigeons are scattered during much of their summer feeding. This starts to change in August, especially in the later weeks, when the cascara starts to ripen. Flocks form, notable cascara groves are selected, and very large concentrations start to appear.

I knew of a canyon in the Coast Range between Pedee and Kings Valley, Oregon, that yearly hosted a multitude of pigeons feeding on cascara. The canyon walls are steep and dotted with dead fir snags rising above the cascara. The bandtails always staged in these dead snags before dropping down to feed. The backdrop behind these snags is pure coastal Northwest: a carpet of endless green, frequently with smoky ground fog during the early mornings.

In 1976 I formulated a plan. A few years previously I had been very impressed by some photographers who constructed a tower next to the nest of a swallow-tailed kite in Florida. The photographs they were able to obtain were brilliant, even better. I decided to take their example and try it for bandtail photos. I wanted to photograph a flock settling into the top of a dead snag, with the backdrop of the Coast Range and the morning mist. I still do.

There was one dead snag that pigeons used on a daily basis for the fifteen years I had known of the canyon. My guess is that they used the snag prior to that also. Up the steep slope were a few live, healthy Douglas firs above the snag. My plan was to make a tower up the side of one of those firs. To do so I rented scaffolding from a masonry contractor and paid the extra charge to have their truck deliver it to the canyon.

My first problem was that the only way into the canyon was

up a very old skid road. The truck driver was unsure whether he wanted to risk trying to get the heavy truck to where I needed the scaffolding unloaded. It took several minutes of serious discussion to win him over. The key seemed to be when I dropped the name of *National Geographic Magazine*. I was certain, once successful with my pigeon photographs, the editors would jump at the chance to print them, just as they did the swallow-tailed kite photos I was so struck with.

It was real touch-and-go getting the truck up the canyon's slope, but he did it. Before he left the driver warned me I'd better get the project over with quickly because, if it rained, no truck on earth would get back there and I would have to carry each section of scaffolding out to the main road, which was about a mile and a half away.

I don't like heights, so at about twenty feet up, my will to construct the scaffolding faltered. I came back the next day with two friends and they completed the project. I was up about forty feet. The next morning before daylight I managed to climb to the top and attach my net blind. I was full of confidence, but I should have known better.

A few months before, I had gone out with an Oregon State University team a few times. They were cannon-netting bandtails for tagging purposes. From those field experiences I should have learned that pigeons very often prove to be uncooperative with the best of plans. The success with cannon-netting varied widely, seemingly centered on the whims of the pigeons. The Oregon State researchers had even rigged a mounted bandtail on a block of wood with wheels from a toy tractor that could be moved around the ground by a length of string. The idea was to lure the pigeons down out of the trees. They didn't buy it.

As for me up on my tower, in the three days I spent swaying to the point of being queasy and fighting a steady flight of aggressive fall yellow jackets, not a single pigeon lit in the dead snag that they had favored for nearly two decades. Instead, they seemed glued to a snag up the canyon that I had never seen them use before. I had to wait nearly twenty years before getting a photograph of a band-tailed pigeon into *National Geographic*, and that one was taken at ground level.

However, I did get to watch the pigeons' feeding pattern for three days, and that somewhat overshadowed the keen disappointment of the whole tower failure. While they avoided the snag, they had no problem with feeding in the cascara all around me. In one case, they were almost directly below me.

Soon after daybreak each morning a large flock moved into the distant snag and the surrounding tops of firs. For the next hour the numbers swelled, with some birds coming from great distances; I could pick them out as faint dots over the ridges. These birds were flying very high and fast, as if they were traveling elsewhere. But once over the canyon, they folded their wings, becoming gray darts as they dropped down in a series of altitude-losing turns. By seven-thirty the fir trees were heavy with pigeons.

Minutes built on slow minutes, and the pigeons sat with apparently no other interest save the enjoyment of the growing warmth of the day. In turn, flocks would shift location from tree to tree in a slow flight, and I would bolt to attention, only to resettle as the pigeons did.

The first feeding always took me by surprise. Even if I was directly watching the pigeons, I was always startled to see a single bandtail suddenly over a cascara. And that first pigeon was followed seconds later by a rush—the branches of the firs springing wildly as they were rid of the weight of the birds. From all directions pigeons came, many from firs far back up on the mountains. They came down in power dives. It was always a moment of pandemonium, made especially intense when compared to the otherwise tranquil pace of the morning.

Bandtail, Mount Jefferson, Oregon

Bandtails alight in a snag, Oregon

Bandtail in a snag, Oregon

Bandtails in Douglas firs, Oregon

Bandtail settling, Oregon

Resting bandtails, Oregon

Bandtail nest and egg, Coast Range, Oregon

Fourteen-day-old bandtail squab, Coast Range, Oregon

Red elderberry

Mineral spring, Oregon

Bandtails drinking at a mineral spring, Oregon

Bandtails at a seashore site, British Columbia

Bandtails at a mineral spring, Oregon Photo by Margaret Thompson Mathewson

Bandtails at a seashore site, Siletz Bay, Oregon

Wes Batterson in Oregon's Coast Range

James Parks, Elk City, Oregon Photo by Ron Cooper

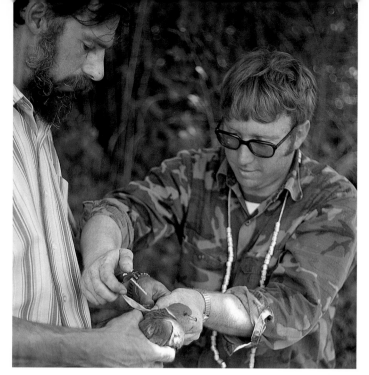

Dr. Robert Jarvis (left) and Mike Passmore banding bandtails

Mike Passmore releasing a banded pigeon

The author hunting bandtails, Coast Range, Oregon Photo by Margaret
Thompson Mathewson

Bandtail hunting

For all the chaos displayed in such feedings—pigeons milling from tree to tree, many descending together on a single branch, the near-thunder crack of many wings clapping, and an oft-heard, much-used, low guttural growl that is thought to be a warning note to other pigeons, reminding them of territorial rights concerning food—the brevity of the feeding period can seem odd. Sometimes, even before the last few stragglers have reached the feed trees, the entire flock lifts with a roar of clapping wings and returns to the taller trees. And so the process is repeated throughout the day. The most frequent feedings take place in the early mornings, and those in the afternoon are separated by progressively longer periods of resting.

Most often I have first heard, rather than seen, flocks of band-tailed pigeons feeding. Once I was nearly a quarter mile away. In fact, at such feeding rushes the band-tailed pigeon can act very much like a parrot. The family of pigeons and doves, *Columbidae*, and that of parrots and parakeets, *Psittacidae*, evolved during the Eocene, which is recognized as the inception of all avian orders present today. The family *Columbidae* is older than the *Psittacidae*. Yet the two are closely related, and there are many similar traits between them.

The first flock of wild parakeets that I saw in flight, in Australia, I mistook at first glance for doves. The same held true in the jungles on the Yucatan-Belize border some years later. And in the Kaimanawa Mountains of New Zealand, where I spent a year, the slow yet powerful flight of the parrot kaka and the New Zealand pigeon looked very much alike from a distance.

Band-tailed pigeons and parrots are most similar in dexterity when feeding in small trees or on branches that bend under their weight. On a few occasions I have purposely hidden under feed trees to watch bandtails. Their parrotlike actions are most noticeable when the feeding is fast paced and competition between birds is great. At this time bandtails often flip upside down to reach the berries or acorns. They do not have the true prolonged walking powers of parrots when in this posture, but with the help of flapping wings they come very close. I once timed a band-tailed pigeon that stayed inverted for fifty-three seconds.

During mid-September, when migration is in full progress in Washington and Oregon, the feeding can be even more hurried. Certain areas attract large numbers of bandtails for a day or two. Then the birds either consume most of the available food and move on or simply leave. In Oregon I have learned to expect the last flocks of the season to be feeding on blue elderberry. It is over quickly. Where just a few weeks before there were smoky blue clouds of bandtails, now there are few. And just as quickly there will be none. It is the time when the Steller's jays reclaim their place as the most noticeable bird in the timber.

A Drink of Salt

Altoona. Pigeon Point springs were visited August 16, 1992. The survey was conducted from 0700 to 1200 hrs. The morning began as overcast, but turned clear and sunny by 1000 hrs. A total of 93 band-tailed pigeons were seen flying into the area of the springs, 111 pigeons were seen either leaving or flying through, and 67 was the greatest number of pigeons counted at one time. Estimate for the band-tailed population at this site is from 67–111.

There are two seeps separated by 40 m along a bluff overlooking the Columbia River. One is little more than a damp area in the clay, and the other seeps into a small pool at the base of the bluff. Both springs are heavily overgrown with briars, bull thistle, wild carrot, and horsetail. Although I saw band-tailed pigeons perching in the alder and Douglas fir surrounding these springs, I did not observe any flying down to seeps. Clearing the vegetation from these springs would perhaps create more favorable habitat for the pigeons.

Climbing the bluff and walking north into the woods I crossed several ravines, two with damp areas that could be mineral sources. Band-tailed pigeon feathers were found as far in as I went, and throughout I could hear occasional soft cooing. No obvious spring was found, but the area may provide nesting habitat for the pigeons. Whether from nesting habitat, multiple mineral sources, or both, the area appears to get a lot of band-tailed pigeon traffic. There was constant flying through by pigeons throughout the survey, and vocalizations were heard from the woods above the bluff. Because of the difficulty in seeing the pigeons the estimate of their numbers at this site may be low.

MEREDITH S. SAVAGE 1993

THE SPRINGS at Altoona, Washington, can't be rated as my favorite among bandtail mineral springs in terms of natural settings. The road into Altoona runs directly by them, and one of the pools is little more than a roadside ditch. But in terms of the band-tailed pigeon and Northwest natives, I will never forget Altoona because of Inez Glazier. She lived down the road in a little cottage next to an old salmon-netting shed. I visited Altoona on July 30, 1974. I greatly wanted to see the steep bluff above the major spring. I had read that the bandtails hung on the nearly vertical walls to drink from the seeps that formed the spring. The result was said to momentarily tinge the bluff's walls blue with pigeons. I had hoped to see that. Instead, all the pigeons sat in the surrounding firs the entire time I stayed.

I found Inez by knocking on doors and asking about pigeons. Everybody knew of them, few knew much else. But Inez certainly knew the band-tailed pigeon. She had been born in Altoona in 1896 and never left. She had seen the bluff's walls "blue with pigeons" many times. And as a girl she told me that she had to be careful when riding her mare near the bluff. Startled pigeons make a loud clap with their wings, and the result never failed to spook the horse. She also said that there weren't many any more. Did I know what had happened to them?

No one seems to know the real reason why bandtails prefer mineral water to the plain stuff, but they are really drawn to it whenever it's available.

JOHN HIGLEY, *Field & Stream* 1980

OVER THE YEARS, I have spent a lot of time viewing mineral springs and seashore sites used by bandtails. There are still many left to see, and I peck away at them each year. When I first checked into the known Washington mineral sites used by band-tails, in November 1973, I was made aware of ten sites by Robert Jeffrey of Washington's Department of Game. In his letter he pointed out that the list was incomplete, particularly with regard to seashore sites. But he also mentioned that the department was considering purchasing eight sites "as money becomes available." The department already owned the Jenny Creek spring and partially owned the Cedar Creek spring.

With some more research I found eight additional sites in Washington. The ten that Jeffrey listed were Cavanaugh Road in Skagit County, St. Martin in Skamania County, Newaukum in Lewis County, Green River in Cowlitz County, Cedar Creek and Jenny Creek in Clark County, Pigeon Bluff in Wahkaikum County, Outlet Creek in Klickitat County, Warm Beach in Snohomish County, and Sumas in Whatcom County. In Oregon, a list compiled in the mid-1950s recorded thirty-six mineral springs and seashore sites:

COUNTY	MINERAL SPRING OR SEASHORE SITE
Benton	Kesters
	Pigeon Butte
	Sulphur Spring
	Twin Pines
Clackamas	Austin Hot Springs
Columbia	Birkenfeld
	Dutch Canyon
Coos	Cooston
	Isthmus Slough
	Prosper
	Russel Point
	Shinglehouse Slough
	Smith River

COUNTY	MINERAL SPRING OR SEASHORE SITE
Curry	Winchuck River
Lane	Camas Swale
	Central
	Cheshire
	Cushman
	London
Lincoln	Drift Creek
	Nashville
Linn	Crawfordsville
	Middle Fork
	Tub Run
	Waterloo
Marion	Aurora
Multnomah	Troutdale
Polk	Grande Ronde
	Salt Creek
	West Monmouth
	Whittakers
Tillamook	Nehalem
	Nestucca
Yamhill	Fairdale
	Panther Creek
	Silver Springs

By the 1970s Oregon's list of springs or tidal areas had been increased to forty-five. In British Columbia nearly all bandtails use tidal areas, as do some of the nesting bandtails in northern California. In British Columbia there are a few inland mineral springs used by the pigeons, such as the Hatzic Spring in the Fraser Valley. California also has inland sites, such as the French

Gulch Spring in Shasta County and the Bangor Spring in Butte County. The exact number of mineral springs and major sea-shore sites used by bandtails in the Northwest is still unknown. During the past several decades much interest has been focused on finding them. For example, in the 1990s Todd Sanders spent a great amount of time and increased Oregon's total number by 73 sites, from 45 to 118. And I know of at least two he missed.

It is important to keep in mind that the Pacific race of band-tails, *Patagioenas fasciata monilis*, is totally dependent upon mineral intake from springs or seashore sites. These pigeons integrate the breeding and nesting period with daily visits to saline waters. Because of a diet during the breeding season that does not sole-ly consist of berries, the interior race *P. fasciata fasciata*, displays little or no interest in such water. What is in these waters that the Northwest pigeons find all important? The ions differ from spring to spring, but basically six minerals are present in all of those sampled. In California, the two well-known springs, French Gulch Spring and Bangor Spring, were analyzed and contained the six minerals in these concentrations (of the six, pay attention to the sodium, as its importance will become evident later):

MINERAL	FRENCH GULCH SPRING (MG/L)	BANGOR SPRING (MG/L)
Calcium	1140	57
Magnesium	7	18
Sodium	3505	936
Chlorine	6635	492
Sulfate	1074	230
Bicarbonate	45	292

Regarding the mineral springs, most in the Northwest are well inland from the coast, some almost a hundred miles. Near the

Pacific bandtails use the estuaries, drinking from pools formed by the high water of the tides. In some locales they drink directly from the surf or patrol the beaches to pick up small crystals of salt.

The bandtail population on British Columbia's Vancouver Island is the foremost of all that I have sought out for their use of beaches. Near Comox, on the east side of the island, on the main highway between Victoria and Campbell River, is a wide, clean gravel beach that plays host to bandtails. Their groups swell in the tops of firs with first morning light, and in late August, when the air is cool and the wind has yet to start blowing across the Georgia Straits, they are a striking sight to watch.

Like all bandtails at mineral springs or tidal areas, they are prone to linger, then come down in a rush, drink, then rush off, with a wild nature directly contrasting with the easy approach into the firs an hour or so before. At this location I have watched pigeons—all members of the same arriving flock—either quickly drink directly from the laps of the waves or search for salt on the small rocks. Oddly, those that drink appear extremely skittish, while those pecking around appear as tame as park pigeons under a bench.

Each year I try to visit new springs or tidal areas. Nearly all of these have local color, and some seep as much Northwest history as the mineral waters they hold. For those interested in watching bandtails, such sites offer an unparalleled opportunity. I certainly have some favorites for pigeon watching. Ideally, one should be afforded a clear view of the surrounding terrain. I prefer to arrive at the site before the sun rises, then watch for the first distant dots. The first flight is comprised of males. Most often they appear as singles or pairs. But there will also be flocks, and depending on how many bandtails are using the spring or tidal area, some of these flocks can be large.

One of my favorite springs for pigeon watching is in Oregon's

Willamette Valley, roughly halfway between the cities of Monmouth and Corvallis. It is located far out in an open field, with only a few small trees to mark it. An old rusty well casing remains from the attempt to find water. The water was salty, so the well was abandoned without being capped. From the rusty casing a steady bubbling of water flows, then forms into a deep, clear pool the size of a bathtub. Some of the pigeons drink from the casing itself, surrounding the pipe and pressing their bills into the flow. Others drink directly from the pool.

In the distance are the foothills of the Coast Range. I always strain my eyes looking for the first of the pigeons to appear from them. The birds come remarkably fast and very high for most of the way until nearly over the spring. Then they tuck their wings in tight and come down in power dives. The entire event is accented with speed and urgency.

But then they wait. And wait. They alight in the surrounding trees and appear to have totally forgotten what they came to the location for. They spend a great deal of time doing nothing. A few may hoot from time to time. A few will growl as they do when in feed trees. If a northern harrier is patrolling the field and comes close to the trees, the pigeons will explode with a roar

that can be heard from a great distance, circle wildly for a while, then lazily sail back to reclaim their perches.

At my favorite spring, while the pigeons are loafing in the trees, large flocks of lesser goldfinches frequently sweep in like a carpet of yellow, drink, and disperse in a blink. If the day is overcast, the duration of tree sitting for the pigeons is longer. On hot days they generally come down after about an hour. And when they do, the rush is on. As with feeding, a single bird drops down. After that a cloud of pigeons heads earthward. The drinking is done quickly, with birds pushing each other for space. In most cases during July, August, and early September the drinking will take place about 7:00 a.m. If one stays around, there will be a second flight around 9:00, this one made up almost entirely of females. Once they are finished, they rise and are quickly lost from view into the foothills again. It is suddenly strangely quiet.

Of all the springs and tidal areas in the Northwest used by bandtails, one of the easiest sites for interested people to watch the pigeons is located in Mt. Rainer National Park. Across from the central hub of the park's headquarters, the restaurant, gift stores, and gas pumps is a series of mineral springs. They are located in a marshy spot named Longmire Meadow. A large flock of bandtails drinks from these springs during July, August, and early September. There is a footpath that circles the marsh; one can stand or sit in the confines of the surrounding forest to watch their morning drink.

Bandtails generally begin to use mineral springs and seashore sites during late June. In most cases they have been back from their wintering grounds for two months prior to this. It was long known that the bandtail in the Northwest starts serious breeding in late June, so the fact that they start appearing at mineral sites at the same time should have offered many a clue as to the reason. Oddly, for many years it didn't.

I personally was most amazed that Arthur S. Einarsen didn't make the connection. Einarsen was certainly among the most talented naturalists who made his life work in the Northwest. Active from the 1930s into the 1960s, he wrote important books such as *The Pronghorn Antelope and Its Management* (1948) and *Black Brant Sea Goose of the Pacific Coast* (1965). Einarsen first worked in the field as a biologist with the U.S. Bureau of Biological Survey (forerunner of the U.S. Fish and Wildlife Service) and then at the Oregon Cooperative Wildlife Research Unit, established at Oregon State University in Corvallis.

Yet in 1946 when Einarsen reported on the hunting taking place at the famous Crawfordsville spring along the Calapooia River in Oregon, he termed the area a pigeon "roost":

> The pigeon area on the Carter farm approximates 40 acres. It is a hill slope, one of the rolling hills of the Cascade foothill area. The lower slopes are grass covered with an occasional dwarfed pine tree and clumps of shrubbery like snowberry or rose briars. Across this slope drains a spring seep. It is known as a "sody" spring, although to taste, its waters are apparently no different that that of other springs in the valley. It is said the pigeons come there to drink, yet in our history no birds have ever been seen at the spring itself, actually drinking. They come to roost in the trees near at hand, and in the early morning flights through the area are great. This occurs all through the summer, but the real concentration does not begin to form until about the middle of August, and then the number of birds using the area is beyond understanding.

I will admit to being embarrassed by Einarsen's report. In fact, I almost wish I had never run across it. Like most people, I have my heroes, and most are those individuals who did wildlife-related work prior to my birth. Arthur Einarsen is certainly at the top of my hero list. Just why he thought that the bandtails were coming into the Crawfordsville spring at 6:00 and 7:00 in the morning to "roost" is beyond me. And the fact that he mentions that the pigeons weren't seen to come down to the spring to drink certainly was due to the one hundred plus shooters blasting away at them while he was there. If this report was made by anyone other than Arthur Einarsen, I would quickly place a "duh" on it.

Oregon State University has been foremost in band-tailed pigeon research. Under Dr. Howard M. Wight and Dr. Robert Jarvis, students have completed important work toward a better understanding of the pigeon. In 1968 Leonard Harold Sisson wrote a thesis entitled "Calling Behavior of Band-Tailed Pigeons in Reference to a Census Technique." In 1969 Gene Donald Silovsky's thesis was on "Distribution and Mortality of the Pacific Coast Band-Tailed Pigeon." In 1970 Daniel M. Keppie completed his thesis, "The Development and Evaluation of an Audio-Index Technique for the Band-Tailed Pigeon." In 1971 Don Leslie Zeigler published "Crop-Milk Cycles in Band-Tailed Pigeons and Loss of Squabs Due to Hunting Pigeons in September."

With the first real research done on the band-tailed pigeon being completed as the result of Oregon State University's interest, a question rose to the top. What are the pigeons doing at the mineral springs and seashore sites? Happily, part of the answer came in 1977 when Michael Forrest Passmore completed his thesis, "Utilization of Mineral Sites by Band-Tailed Pigeons."

Through banding and wing tagging, researchers learned that pigeons likely formed loose colonies around the various mineral sites and visited them daily during the peak of the breeding season, from late June to early September. Additional research by Passmore, Jarvis, G. L. March, and R. M. F. S. Sadleir suggested it was calcium that the pigeons sought in the waters. This made sense because calcium is important to the bandtail for egg production, but even more so for the formation of pigeon milk produced in the crop to feed the very young squab. It was felt that the breeding-season total-berry diet of the bandtail in the Northwest lacked the calcium needed, so that the visits to the springs and seashore sites supplemented that mineral.

And to a degree this was true. Pigeons do get a boost in calcium from some waters, but certainly not all. In 1999 Todd A. Sanders completed "Habitat Availability, Dietary Mineral Supplement, and Measuring Abundance of Band-Tailed Pigeons in Western Oregon," his Ph.D. dissertation at Oregon State. It had been determined by Jarvis and Passmore that Pacific Northwest bandtails fed on red elderberry almost exclusively from late June to mid-August, and then almost solely on cascara berries from late August into early September. Sanders and Jarvis found that bandtails feeding only on these berries may be 2–5 times deficient in calcium (depending on calcium requirement), 5–75 times deficient in sodium (depending on berry species consumed), and 2–9 times high in potassium (depending on berry species consumed and potassium requirement).

However, Sanders was puzzled when he sampled a host of Oregon springs and tidal areas. Some with very heavy pigeon use measured very low in calcium. While extra intake of calcium in the locations where it was present was an aid to the pigeon, it apparently wasn't the real reason the bird needed the mineral waters. What he came up with was interesting indeed (Sanders 1999):

> The diet of Band-tailed Pigeons feeding exclusively on elder and cascara berries can be particularly deficient in sodium, but it also contains a sodium and potassium cation electrolyte imbalance. The required potassium:sodium

ratio ranges from 2.0 to 4.7 in poultry. The potassium:sodium ratio in the diet of Band-tailed Pigeons while consuming red elder was 137.6, and increased to 656.3 when they switched to cascara. Electrolyte balance in a bird's intracellular and extracellular fluids is critical for cellular functions and for osmotic and acid-base relationships. Absorption and retention of sodium can be lessened by excessive potassium intake. As a consequence of the sodium and potassium cation imbalance in berries of elder and cascara, Band-tailed Pigeons may seek a dietary sodium supplement to balance their cationic electrolyte imbalance, or satisfy their sodium deficiency associated with potassium loading.

In other words, the band-tailed pigeons are killing themselves with a potassium overload and need to balance it with a drink of good, strong sodium every day during their berry diet. And they have paid dearly for this requirement. Since the first white settlers came to the Northwest, it has been known that the place to shoot pigeons is at mineral water.

To the South and Back

Periods and routes of migration of the bandtails are strongly influenced by availability of food and weather phenomena, especially temperature and rainfall. Owing to the vast areas of wilderness thorough which the birds pass, it is difficult to trace their movements, and over much of their range they appear to move in small flocks which often may pass unnoticed.

JOHNSON A. NEFF 1947

OVER THE YEARS I have seen the largest number of bandtails during their September migration through Oregon. In times past the numbers have been heartwarming. And I have certainly looked for them in numbers elsewhere. During the time when I used to travel to Vancouver Island in late August and early September for sea-run cutthroat and Chinook salmon fishing and during a short period when I lived on the upper end of Lake Cowichan at Youbou, British Columbia, I spent a disproportionate amount of time watching, or trying to watch, bandtails.

I did see bandtails in good numbers in a dozen or more locales on Vancouver Island. But in most cases these sightings were made in late August. I recall seeing large flocks at the Oyster River, Maple Bay, Lake Cowichan, Cowichan Bay, along Nitinat Lake, and along the mountainous portion of the main highway, north of Victoria. However, by the first week of September, I saw only scattered flocks, and small ones at that, in many of the same areas. I was left with the impression that the pigeons had departed for the south.

A generalization could be made that bandtails leave British Columbia in late August, Washington during the second week of September, and roughly the northern half of Oregon by the third week of September. These dates can vary by a week or more depending on the year, weather conditions, and of course most important, food availability. But overall one is very safe in saying that by October 1 most Northwest bandtails are in northern California, on the way to their wintering grounds in the central and southern parts of the state.

Johnson A. Neff, author of the most authoritative work ever done on the bandtail, *Habits, Food, and Economic Status of the Band-Tailed Pigeon* (1947), followed the migration in 1937 in Oregon. This very interesting and challenging project began in late August in Tillamook County, on the northern Oregon coast. Neff moved with the pigeons southward, staying along the coast. By mid-September the birds were still grouped in the middle section of the state. By September 29 the migration had moved south of Coquille into the then vast, timbered, nearly roadless belt that lay on the Oregon-California border. There he lost track of the birds.

But at the same time Arthur Einarsen was inland, serving in part as an aid to Neff. He reported a heavy concentration of pigeons in the Rogue River Valley during late September, north of the point where Neff had halted. Of interest, several weeks later, Einarsen reported seeing a few bandtails in the same area. His sightings were October 19–23.

This late October Rogue Valley sighting was very likely made up of straggling pigeons, commonly seen drifting south long after the major migration has passed. There are also some bandtails that winter over as far north as Vancouver Island. Most of these depend on backyard bird feeders and are few in number. However, in mid-December 1961, I walked out of a Salem, Oregon, grocery store and saw forty or more bandtails feeding in a madrona tree white with frost.

At one time, before the drastic decline in the band-tailed pigeon population in the early 1970s, it was possible to see very large flocks of migrating pigeons. Arthur Einarsen reported seeing nearly a thousand pigeons in 1944 at a point on the Cowlitz River in southern Washington. That sighting amounted to a lot of birds, and more interesting was the date—September 25. It must have been a late migration that year, as generally the birds would have been more than three hundred miles further south by that date.

Another interesting question surrounding the migration, as yet unanswered, is which of the two mountain ranges does the Pacific race use for migration? There are clearly two well-defined paths, the Coast Range and the Cascades, which provide an unbroken timbered highway from British Columbia into California. In most locations, about seventy miles separate the two. While it is not certain if one range supports more migrating pigeons than the other, ask ten bandtail experts and they will likely give the edge to the Coast Range. Much of this will be due to the large population of nesting pigeons found along the coast.

Having stated that, I will go on record in saying that my nod would also go to the Coast Range route, but the largest concentrations of pigeons I have ever seen have been in the Cascade Mountains. Seeing pigeons in flocks between 250 and 300 birds constitutes a lot of bandtails in one place at one time, and I have seen such concentrations only a few times.

But my whopper, that sighting of a lifetime, took place in mid-September 1965 in the Cascades above the Clackamas River in northern Oregon. A friend and I had climbed up on a ridge overlooking the river during late afternoon. Near the top we flushed nearly an entire mountainside of pigeons. They were feeding on blue elderberry, and we sat on logs to watch. I have never seen, nor am likely ever again to see, as many bandtails. From our vantage point we could see far to the north and down the river to the south. There were bandtails in both directions and at all points in between. And they were moving.

Some flocks flew across the river's canyon to our side. But most traded steadily southward. Some settled in tall firs briefly, but were soon in the air again, leaving the fir tops in power dives and appearing as sudden explosions of soft gray confetti against a backdrop of green. In the two hours we sat and watched, I am certain that the number of pigeons we saw approached 1500, perhaps more.

In regard to band-tailed pigeon movements during migration, I knew a location in the Coast Range where the pigeons appeared and disappeared like clockwork. For more than twenty years, before the canyon was sold to a large timber company and cleared to plant young firs, the pigeons were there. From an aesthetic standpoint the site was truly a classic. Maybe it was the most beautiful ridge and canyon in the entire Coast Range. (It was the place where I once tried to photograph the pigeons from a tower without success.) The sole attraction for the pigeons was cascara. The trees grew in amazing groves on the lower walls of the canyon. A clear, slow-running stream, blocked in numerous places by sprawling beaver dams, flowed though the canyon's floor. My guess is that nearly a mile of creek bottom on both sides was largely made up of cascara.

I would walk up on the main ridge above the canyon on old, nearly overgrown skid roads. In places they made sharp switchbacks through a standing fir forest before breaking out on the ridge. From that vantage point I was able to look down on the pigeons far below. At the height, I have seen more than five hundred pigeons in that canyon. But the timing was nothing short of remarkable; I saw the birds, each and every year, at the same time.

In most years the cascara berries would be ripe during the last week of August, or almost so. Bandtails have no druthers about eating cascara berries while green, so whether they are ripe or not has no bearing. This canyon is within some of the major bandtail breeding areas in Oregon's eastern slope of the Coast Range. A large mineral spring, all important to breeding bandtails, the Nashville Spring, is about eighteen miles to the south of this canyon.

Yet even with the limbs of the cascara trees sagging under the weight of the berries, I rarely, if ever, saw any pigeons in this canyon during the first two weeks of September. The date I marked on my calendar was September 17. I lost track of how many years the pigeons seem to appear on or very near that date. By September 22 the flocks had always reached their peaks. Just two or three days later, they were almost entirely gone. Some years, so were the cascaras. But in other years enough berries were left on the trees to support the pigeons nearly another week, had they wished to stay. But they never did, leaving a setting of solitude broken only by Steller's jays and the pine squirrels hurriedly cutting the last of their fir cones for winter.

In 1958 I found, by chance and luck, a unique feeding area that supported migrating pigeons very near the then city limits of Salem, Oregon. From that time until the mid-1970s I saw pigeons there yearly. (Today the ridge has been cleared and a large winery has been developed.) I found the place out of curiosity. I had become intrigued regarding the origin of a spasmodic evening flight of bandtails that worked along high ridges with enough regularity that I could count on seeing them during the first part of September. This evening flight never failed to appear, coming from a ridge to the south. In 1957 I tried to find the source—if in fact there was one.

I didn't walk far enough the first year, but the second year I did. About five miles to the south from where I had first seen the flights, I found what turned out to be a truly remarkable feeding area for bandtails. It was one I have never seen equaled due to the variety of foods present, all eaten by the pigeons.

The entire area was no more than thirty acres. It was situated on a high ridge top that was crowned by a tall, thick, but small stand of large Douglas firs. Below the fir forest lay a slope of scrub forest, a tangle of vine maple, assorted other small hardwoods, and a few large spreading white oaks. Added to this was a cover of almost impregnable underbrush, bound together by a vast interlocking mass of blackberry vines. The only way to get around on the slope was via black-tailed deer paths, and frequently it was a hands-and-knees affair.

On this hillside grew all four of the bandtail's principal fall foods in Oregon: cascara, Pacific dogwood, blue elderberry, and in some years white oak acorns. Over many years I watched them consume all three—sometimes four foods when the oaks had acorns—in the course of a month in rapid succession. In early September the pigeons would start with cascara until they had eaten the last berry. Then they would move on to dogwood, and during two years that I saw, white oak acorns. They would end with the blue elderberry.

But it was the number of bandtails, tied directly to their annual buildup at this location, that made a lasting impression. I could clearly see migrating pigeons arrive. By the last week of August and the first week of September, there was always a sizeable flock feeding on the hillside. The number frequently reached fifty birds, which fed solely on the cascara. There weren't as many cascara trees as there were dogwood and blue elderberry, so the pigeons went through the berries quickly.

During the second week of September the setting underwent a marked population upswing. In some years the number of bandtails soared to almost three hundred. Feeding in this week in September was based around the dogwood berries, and it always proved to be an outstanding week to watch the pigeons. They had competition for the berries. Along with the band-tailed pigeons were large flocks of robins and cedar waxwings, all wildly feeding. At times the small, squat dogwoods shook from the number of birds in their branches.

Once most of the dogwood berries were gone, the pigeons started in on the blue elderberries. But oddly, they didn't feed for long on these. By the third week of September, with bushels of elderberries left untouched, the birds vanished nearly overnight. This tight schedule didn't vary much from year to year.

It was always of great interest to me that this area is almost directly in the center of the Willamette Valley, equal in distance from the Coast Range to the west and the Cascades to the east. I feel there is little question that the pigeons I saw in late August and early September were local nesting birds, as once many bandtails nested on the ridges within the valley. But where the sudden buildup in the population came from always caused me to wonder. I wish I knew. In all likelihood it was simply a movement directly down the valley, perhaps from the hills surrounding the Portland area, where bandtails once nested in numbers. Or perhaps the swell in numbers represented a shift inland from either major mountain range highway, as the bandtail is a very mobile traveler. It leaves a trail of question marks as it goes.

The return migration in the spring is somewhat different. The pigeons aren't in a hurry. Wes Batterson told me that he commonly saw some bandtails in April, at times as early as March, in the nesting areas around his northern Oregon coastal home. But he started to see large numbers in early May.

Nearly all California reports indicate that the wintering pigeons shift into their northward movement in February and

March and are absent from the wintering grounds by April. Depending on the food supplies, this spring migration can be a leisurely one, with large flocks frequenting regions for a while before continuing north. This almost casual approach to northward movement is not unlike the changing of the Northwest seasons, with spring blending into early summer in stages. By June the band-tailed pigeon is firmly back in the Northwest, and the region is richer as a result.

A New Predator

It is said that the band-tailed pigeon remains together in moderate sized flocks after the nesting season, are sometimes seen in numbers innumerable, and are often slaughtered by the score. Let the people of the Northwest have a care, before it is too late.

WILLIAM ROGERS LORD 1902

OREGON'S Willamette Valley begins at the southern end of Portland and terminates approximately a hundred miles to the south in Eugene. The major population centers in the valley are Portland, Salem, Albany/Corvallis, and Eugene. Each center is served by a highway running west to the Pacific. Leaving Portland on Highway 30, one first sees the Pacific at Seaside. As for the three other highways: from Salem, Lincoln City; from Albany/Corvallis, Newport; and from Eugene, Florence. Three of the four highways, 18, 20, and 126, are archaic, built for the traffic flow of fifty or more years ago, certainly not for the stream of people frequently driving to spend time on the beaches today. In a desperate attempt to relieve congestion and reduce danger, the highway department has widened some sections of these old roads. But largely the pavement snakes through the Coast Range like the narrow, old logging roads they were formed from.

Highway 20, from Albany/Corvallis, is likely the most serpentine, and there are thirty-mile-an-hour curves in places. One such curve, entered from the east, suddenly deposits the traveler in downtown Eddyville. Head around another curve, over the railroad tracks, and Eddyville is passed.

This little coastal hamlet will always have lasting memories for me. For one, I once passed through Eddyville and a young boy was standing on the roadside selling copies of *Grit*. This was during the early 1970s and it flashed me back to the 1950s, when ads in comic books and the scout magazine, *Boy's Life*, urged us to sell this little newspaper and earn money or prizes.

Then there was the goat. It was there for several years. Driving west I saw it on the left, chained securely in the front yard of the third or fourth house in Eddyville. It was a huge billy with horns. His muscles were so pronounced he appeared as though carved from stone. He was a dirty yellow-brown, and the hair on his lower neck, back, and butt stood angrily straight up, like an oafish redneck with a fresh crew cut. But it was the goat's eyes that transfixed the viewer. They were cold, dull yellow, and simply smoldered with pure hate. That goat was, and still is, the meanest looking animal I have ever seen.

Aside from these memories—and far more important—Eddyville will be of lasting importance to me because of band-tailed pigeons. In the wonderful book *Birds of America*, first published in 1917, William L. Finley wrote of the bandtail and Eddyville: "Mr. O. G. Dalaba of Corvallis, Oregon, says that he caught a great many in the coast hills in the early nineties. He says he got twenty-five dozen birds at one spring of the net at Eddyville and many others got away."

Curious about Finley's reference, I stopped in Eddyville in the late 1960s and began research by knocking on doors. I was looking for the oldest resident in town. It turned out that he lived back up the road a few miles, and his name was Mr. Brown Wakefield. Our meeting proved to be the start of a mother lode of information. Mr. Wakefield was in his seventies, had lived on his farm his entire life, and, yes, he recalled mention of people trapping wild pigeons for market, but didn't know anything about any fellow named Dalaba from Corvallis.

He said the pigeons were trapped in the large pasture next to town, but that is all he knew for sure. He could tell me all sorts of things that happened around Eddyville, such as when the train came up from Newport and brought the mail, along with the daily paper. The engineer would throw the papers from the train as it passed houses. A Mr. Irving had a dog that would get the paper and bring it back to the house. But on the day that President McKinley was shot, the dog buried the paper.

"Why don't you go over to Elk City and speak with Jim Parks? He would likely know more about it than I do," Mr. Wakefield suggested.

Jim Parks certainly did! He was ninety-two when I spoke with him, clear eyed and sharp, both in memory and manner. He had lived on the homestead up the Big Elk River since he was a small child. He was born in Arkansas in 1877 and came to Oregon in 1879 when his father, Leander Parks, came west with horse and wagon. Mr. Parks didn't know anything about pigeons at Eddyville, nor anyone by the name of Finley or Dalaba, and had never heard of *Birds of America*, but did know something about trapping "blue wild pigeons."

Starting in the late 1880s, his father and W. N. Lansdell trapped bandtails every spring. Jim Parks remembered very well helping them, because the cedar boxes they built to ship the birds were so heavy when full that he couldn't pick them up. Nearly all the trapping was done during the 1890s up until about 1905.

His father and Lansdell trapped pigeons during the spring, generally late April and into May. They did so by plowing a small field in the timber and baiting it with wheat. A net was used, being thrown by freshly cut vine maples. He said the maple cuttings needed to be replaced frequently because they lost their spring.

Parks said that they didn't try to trap every day. Instead, over a period of about three weeks, they trapped about twice a week. A good throw of the net would bring them sixty to eighty "blue wild pigeons." Cedar boxes were built to hold the birds, and once a week they took the pigeons to Elk City, where a flat-bottomed scow took the birds down the Yaquina River to Newport. From there they were put on an ocean steamer bound for San Francisco.

While netting bandtails in the Northwest was certainly practiced, shooting them for market was far more common. In 1887 a hunter named Phil Baltimore was reported to have shot seventy-five bandtails in one day, including five with one shot. The location was given as "in the hills above Crawfordsville." This Crawfordsville reference is of some importance, as it is the earliest one I have found about killing pigeons in the region around the very notable mineral spring at Crawfordsville. There are later accounts from the 1890s that state that the pigeons killed at Crawfordsville were taken to Albany, then sent by rail to Portland and market.

Most market hunting in the West centered around waterfowl. But deer were certainly sought, as were upland birds, most notably the valley quail in California. Band-tailed pigeons were eagerly killed whenever and however possible.

During the winter of 1911–1912 wintering pigeons took advantage of a bumper crop of acorns in a relatively small area of California from Paso Robles to Nordhoff. The result was catastrophic for the bandtail. Both market hunters and sport shooters responded to the vast flocks that concentrated there. In the aftermath, W. Lee Chambers wrote the first of many articles on behalf of the bandtail. His first was entitled "Who Will Save the Band-tailed Pigeon?" and it appeared in *Condor*. Chambers's article, reprinted in nearly anything written on the bandtail since, was published during the summer of 1912. In part, he wrote:

> Band-tailed pigeons were abundant this winter from Paso Robles south to Nordhoff all through the coast range of mountains. One hunter from Los Olivos shipped over 2000 birds to the San Francisco and Los Angeles hotels.
>
> The morning train from San Luis Obispo to Los Olivos on Sundays averaged 100 passengers who came to hunt pigeons. A prominent hunter told me that these passengers averaged about thirty birds apiece per day. This would make this one day's excursion over 3000 pigeons. Now!— this is only one train and one day's hunting. One can hardly calculate the number of birds killed by hunters in automobiles and those who started from Los Angeles, San Francisco, Santa Barbara, Ventura, Santa Maria, Paso Robles, Lompoe and other small towns.
>
> It is a shame that something is not done for these beautiful birds, which are doomed to follow in the footsteps of the Passenger Pigeon. I honestly believe that the people will never again see such a flight of Band-tailed Pigeons. In Nordhoff it is the largest they have ever seen, and the birds evidently hung around until they were simply shot out. This same state of affairs is probably true in other localities. If something is not done very quickly these birds are doomed; for any bird that fly in such flocks is bound to be exterminated. What can be done?

Chambers's notice and other reports of the killing brought quick action. A closed season on the band-tailed pigeon in California was advocated by the Cooper Ornithological Club's Permanent Committee on Conservation of Wildlife and made a leading item in the legislative program of the California Associated Societies for the Conservation of Wildlife. At the request of the secretary of the State Fish and Game Commission, Dr. Joseph Grinnell prepared a paper titled "The Outlook for Conserving the Band-tailed Pigeon as a Game Bird of California," which appeared in *Condor* in January 1913. The California legislature accepted the recommendations of the conservationists and passed the bill providing for the closed season. However, the legislation was not signed by the governor and thus failed to become a law. The California agitation on the subject was by no means lost, however, for it undoubtedly furnished the impetus for the adoption of the long closed season by the federal government.

If there is anything good that can be said about the 1911–1912 vast overkill of bandtails, it was timed well. Sweeping wildlife reforms were being adopted, and certainly one of the most important was the Migratory Bird Act of 1913. This act gave the U.S. government the authority over birds "that in the course of their northern and southern migrations passed through any of the States or that did not remain permanently within the borders of any State or Territory." The U.S. Department of Agriculture was given control and was directed to adopt suitable regulations to protect the birds. Among these were establishing limits and seasons for game birds and totally closed seasons for some species. Due to Chambers's outcry on behalf of the bandtail and the powerful aid of famed West Coast ornithologist Joseph Grinnell, the pigeon was provided protection.

The Migratory Bird Act of 1913 was greatly strengthened when the United States and England signed the Migratory Bird Treaty Act on July 3, 1918. This act gave protection to the species migrating between Canada and the United States, and it continued to protect species for which there was concern. Again, band-tailed pigeons were covered by this act, and they would remain protected until 1932. But with protection came growing com-

David Hagerbaumer

plaints about bandtails causing crop damage. Such complaints were certainly nothing new. W. Lee Chambers wrote of pigeon crop damage at the turn of the century in California:

> A very excited man came to my store about February 25, 1900, and told of thousands of wild pigeons being poisoned on the Wolfskill Ranch. The pigeons were eating the grain faster that it could be sowed and harrowed, and the ranch people had scattered some poisoned grain which was killing the birds. I had never seen wild pigeons, so I hurriedly rode my bicycle to the ranch which was near the present site of Sawtelle, then a large barley field.
>
> When I arrived at the field I saw a large flock of turkey vultures feasting on the dead pigeons, the remains and feathers of which covered a large part of 160 acres. I gathered all the perfect birds I could carry in two sacks and rode back to Santa Monica. Harry Swarth made these into beautiful specimens for me on a fifty-fifty basis.
>
> It is impossible for me to estimate how many Band-tailed Pigeons were poisoned, but the original flock must have been a large one. The poisoning and vulture feast

went on all day. I was present only at the end of the inci-
dent. As far as I know this never happened again in the
Santa Monica area, and my notes do not mention pigeons
again up to the time I moved from there.

Prior to the widespread practice of planting grain by drilling
rather than broadcasting and harrowing, bandtails could prove to
be a problem for farmers. But very likely this problem was greatly overstated, at least in the case of grains.

Frank B. Wire, well known in Oregon for his long association with wildlife in the state, among many other things, was a
market hunter during the 1890s and early 1900s. Wire (1960)
wrote about using decoys to hunt bandtails in agricultural fields:

> In the spring the bandtails came north from California
> where they wintered. They did considerable damage to the
> hand-sown spring oats. The farmers begged us to come
> and shoot. We would get a start from a few flocks as they
> flew overhead and then put them out for decoys. We were
> prepared with willow sticks. We would stick the sharpened
> end of the stick into the underside of their head and then
> into the ground. I always carried a pocket full of rubber
> bands, and one of these was put around the body to hold
> the wings together.
>
> If you think that ducks decoy, you should see the pigeons
> come in! As we shot more birds we kept eight or ten in the
> blind, and when we saw a flock headed our way we threw
> them out over the decoys. Sometimes we cut a forked stick
> about four feet long and stuck it into the ground among
> the decoys. We broke both wings of the dead birds so they
> would flap when dropped. A string was tied around the
> bird's neck and run back to the blind. When birds were
> coming in the string was pulled and the bird dropped sev-

eral times. This attracted the birds, as when wild pigeons feed on the fields the ones in the rear fly over those ahead, and they cross a field just like a wave in the ocean.

Nowadays the oats and wheat are sown by drilling it in mechanically, and as pigeons won't scratch, they don't bother grain any more and this source of their feed is taken away. However, they feed on berries and sometimes raid the strawberry patches and the ripening cherries. They will also eat green prunes when they are about the size of a marble.

With the practice of drilling grain seeds into the ground, most complaints of bandtails damaging grain crops ceased. As Wire noted, pigeons don't scratch the ground in the manner of chickens, turkeys, and many other birds. If the seeds are not lying on top of the ground, the pigeons don't get them. After the bandtailed pigeon gained protection in 1913, reports of damage were investigated by wildlife agents.

Some of these reports were likely overstated. In September 1924, for example, a farmer in Sumas, Washington, reported that bandtails were not only eating his newly planted wheat, but pulling up sprouted plants. (The latter is something that bandtailed pigeons don't do.) In the spring of 1925 Ira N. Gabrielson (later coauthor with Stanley G. Jewett of *Birds of Oregon* and chief of the U.S. Bureau of Biological Survey) traveled to Washington after alleged depredations by pigeons on peas. Most of the complaints came from San Juan Island, but Gabrielson found that the pigeons had been picking up the peas left on top of the ground, rather than the ones drilled, thus causing no appreciable damage.

There were, however, a few valid reports of bandtails causing damage to both peas and wheat in the fall before the crops could be harvested. The pigeons were said to light on the stalks and bend them earthward to feed. Johnson Neff carefully reviewed

the bandtail crop damage reports during the 1930s, and con-
cluded in his 1947 report that:

> Depredations on agricultural crops by band-tailed pigeons
> although sporadic may be serious. They are generally local
> and vary greatly from season to season. They sometimes
> involve numbers of birds so large as to be amazing, and
> again may concern only a few pairs. Their occurrence is
> so erratic as to be impossible to forecast, although in some
> areas slight to moderate damage may be done annually.
> The supply of natural wild foods is a determining factor
> in the occurrence of crop damage because of its effects on
> both pigeon concentrations and routes of migration. With
> natural foods plentiful in the mountains and wilderness
> there is less necessity for the pigeons to feed extensively
> on cultivated crops.

Starting in the 1920s complaints about the bandtails increased. Nearly all of these came from individuals with cherry
orchards. In 1924 a grower in Paradise, California, claimed to
have lost 1500 pounds of cherries. In that same year another Paradise grower, stating that he spoke for twenty other growers,
claimed losses from one-fifth to three-fourths of their crop for
three years running. As the 1920s rolled on, the complaints became more frequent. A U.S. game warden named George Tonkin
looked into most of these California reports. In 1926 a cherry
grower at Dunsmuir told him that he lost all but 60 pounds of a
1000-pound crop to band-tailed pigeons. In 1930 a prune grower in Gilroy, California, reported damage amounting to $2,500.

While there were numerous other reports, not only in California, but in Oregon and Washington as well, the one that ulti-
mately proved the turning point for the protection of the bandtail took place in March 1930. On a ranch near Arvin in Kern

County, California, bandtails were blamed for heavy damage to a vineyard. During the previous fall a bumper crop of grapes was not picked. The fruits had dried to raisins, both those still on the vines and the ones on the ground. The pigeons drawn to the area to feed on the raisins were estimated to number 200,000 by two California Division of Fish and Game wardens. The damage was caused by the pigeons lighting on the grape vines and breaking off the new growth. This was truly an enormous, near unbelievable concentration of pigeons, as any number over two or three hundred in one place can be considered huge.

Several plans were undertaken to address the problem. First, 1000 pounds of barley and 500 pounds of raisins were spread away from the vineyard. The pigeons quickly ate all of this and returned to the vineyard. Then an airplane buzzed the vineyard in an attempt to discourage the birds. It didn't work. The ranch owner and the California game wardens hired sixteen men to patrol the vineyard with shotguns. Still the pigeons came. On March 30, fifty men were invited to shoot the pigeons, but still the pigeons returned. On March 31 and April 1, three hundred men came to shoot. On April 2, the number swelled to five hundred, each with about two hundred rounds of ammunition each. The report filed was that "a bombardment such as has not been heard since the First World War took place from daylight to about noon."

Finally, the pigeons departed, leaving behind an estimated 5000 to 7000 dead on the last day. While this case appears to be an example of true bandtail damage to crops, most complaints, once investigated, prove to be largely unfounded. Johnson Neff, who personally became familiar with many of the complaints, summed it up well: "Far too great a percentage of the complaints against the pigeons, as against other game birds, upon close analysis, are found to be unjustified. In many instances the desire

to shoot pigeons will be found to be the underlying motive for the complaint."

Compared with other game birds, the band-tailed pigeon has had but little study. Several important parts of its life history are still unknown, and among these are the pigeon's natural enemies. There isn't anything recorded that points to any serious predation of the bandtail. It has been stated that prairie falcons prey on bandtails. Likewise Cooper's hawks have been seen preying on them. I once watched a Cooper's sneak up on a feeding flock of pigeons in a cascara tree and rush in to grab one in a brown, feathered blink. While Mike Passmore and Robert Jarvis were releasing pigeons they had just banded, a Cooper's hawk took full advantage and struggled off with one it caught just seconds after the pigeon's release.

Other predators would be expected. For example, great horned owls don't pass up anything until it reaches the size of a large raccoon. Steller's jays and ravens likely find nests and young bandtail squabs. In fact, in a rather remarkable account in *Audubon* years ago, someone wrote of watching a pair of ravens outfly a bandtail along the Wind River in Washington and force it to the ground, where the ravens killed it. Pine squirrels and chipmunks would be quick to eat any unguarded egg they encountered. And peregrine falcons have surely stooped pigeons that use coastal tidal flats for their daily drink of salt.

With regard to natural mortality, there is also the matter of the poor nest the band-tailed pigeon constructs, and the fact that eggs and squabs are lost as a result. During a period I had a federal permit to keep bandtails in captivity, my ace-in-the-hole place for obtaining pigeons was the Portland Audubon Society animal shelter. Each summer, especially in August, people would find young bandtail squabs on the ground and bring them to the shelter. All the squabs that I was given were too young to have left the nest on their own.

Perhaps with more investigation into the pigeon's life history, information will surface about the predators they face. But after a hundred years or so of rather limited study, it appears that the bandtail is somewhat unique in that it only really needs to fear one predator—man. In 1932 the band-tailed pigeon was returned to the list of legal game birds that could be shot. The gravest dangers the pigeon had ever faced lay ahead.

Afield with Gun

You cannot follow the wild trails far without the conviction that the human hunter is the cruelest of all the beasts of prey. You cannot follow the sportsman far without foreseeing still longer closed seasons, much stricter regulations of all shooting, and even moral tests, and tests for marksmanship, before men with guns shall be allowed to go without official attendance into the woods. More than that, if you will follow the sportsman far enough, you will lose much of your taste for blood; you will be forced to the conviction that the pursuit of wild things no longer has its legitimate nor its most thrilling consummation in the kill.

DALLAS LORE SHARP 1914

I FIRST READ this passage when I was fourteen. It was written by Dallas Lore Sharp in his book *Where Rolls the Oregon.* In the summer of 1912 Sharp was with William L. Finley near Malheur marsh in eastern Oregon, where he witnessed the shooting and crippling of a coyote. Sharp's words deeply disturbed me. It was the first negative message I had experienced regarding hunting. Forty-six years later it still disturbs me, but perhaps not to the degree it once did. Today it makes me uncomfortable, for there is truth in some of what Sharp wrote.

When I first read Sharp's words I was a young member of a southern sportsman-oriented family. I was exposed to both hunting and fishing in North Carolina and Virginia from my earliest years. And I loved it all, much more than my two brothers and eventually more than my father. Outdoor pursuits—hunting, fishing, and trapping—grew to almost totally take over my life, and as a result I turned to writing about it, both in magazines and books.

Make no mistake, I am a hunter—but a rather specialized one. I have no interest in big game; I hunt only birds. Over the years I have killed a great many, and I hope for many more before my ashes are scattered via shotgun shells by friends who have shared the field with me. Among the birds I have bagged have been band-tailed pigeons. Lots of them. From 1956 until 1975 I hunted the pigeon as if on a mission. I simply loved hunting bandtails in their mountain retreats.

But in train, I came to view other pigeon shooters with the same feelings expressed by those in the past who came to know the pigeon well—feelings of contempt, anger, and grave frustration. The whitest heat of my anger is because most shooters display so little respect for the bird. To them it is "only a pigeon" and therefore does not rate the status of other game birds.

For reasons that I have failed to come to grips with, hunters have always treated pigeons and doves differently than other kinds of birds. This is odd—if that is the correct word—because mourning doves, for example, are shot with near total disregard by the same individuals who practice impeccable sportsmanship when afield for species such as bobwhite quail or ruffed grouse.

Those who don't hunt will likely be puzzled, perhaps irritated, to hear that some hunters love the quarry they kill. Admittedly it is an odd combination of emotions. And, at least for me, it is not easy to explain to those truly interested. Most frequently, I find myself using the bobwhite quail in the South as my example.

For all practical purposes, the bobwhite is now all but gone from much of its former range. The decline began in the 1950s and tragically gained momentum. The quail didn't vanish because of overshooting, however, it vanished because of changes in agriculture. But during the period from George Washington's presidency to the decline, the bobwhite was revered. The bird's lofty status served to build a code of ethics among hunters. This code was powerfully self-enforced by the legions of those who hunted the bird—who, again, deeply loved the quail.

According to this code, unlike other game birds, the bobwhite quail was almost never market hunted. A sportsman never shot one on the ground. Coveys were closely watched, and shooting ceased before half the covey had been bagged. During severe weather, quail hunters rushed feed into the quail covers. Gentlemen shot quail, gentlemen both rich and poor. And gentlemen are *hunters*, not shooters. Or at least for bobwhite quail they were.

With the pigeons and doves, however, it appears nearly all hunters turn into shooters. This attitude is found worldwide. A few years ago, after my book *Reflections on Snipe* was published, I received a long letter from one of North America's better-known bird shooters. At the time I assumed he was a hunter. The letter frankly flattered me and contained an invitation to spend two days with the man in Louisiana in pursuit of snipe.

I was especially interested in doing this because he was a close friend of Gene Hill, one of the most talented writers of angling and hunting material of the past fifty years. Hill, noted for his insight into outdoor pursuits, such as my favorite, "Who ever said money can't buy happiness never bought a Lab puppy," was a man I had always hoped to meet, but he passed away before our trails crossed. The fellow who wrote to me had established a shooting ranch in Mexico, entertained numerous people, and for years Hill made an annual visit. I was eager to get insights into Hill from his host.

I did, but I also quickly came to terms with the type of shooter I had joined in the rice fields near Lake Charles on that foggy

January morning. On the drive out, one of my first questions involved red-billed pigeons. I asked him if he had them on his place in Mexico. I learned that his "best day" that he could recall was seventy-eight killed. Among other things, he also told me of being arrested on some property he owned in Texas for exceeding the limit on mourning doves. He had apparently staged a dove shoot, attended by several dozen shooters, and they had killed more than 1000 doves before enforcement officers arrived on the scene.

Our snipe hunt quickly turned sour. There were hundreds of birds. Two other shooters were present. The limit was eight snipe per day, which all four of us reached quickly. I cased my gun and watched the others continue. My host came over to where I stood and with some irritation informed me that he had promised snipe to a number of people in Houston, and he wanted me to continue shooting. I declined a dinner with the group that evening and excused myself from the affair. What I should have done was reported the violation. I didn't, and I have frequently regretted not doing so.

In the May/June 2003 issue of *Gray's Sporting Journal*, considered by most to be the benchmark of excellence for hunting and fishing literature, there is a full-page ad for eared dove shooting in Argentina. In the ad there is a shooter pictured kneeling on a pile of dead doves, stated to number 7696. It isn't clear how many days it took the individual to kill these. My guess is that it was done in the standard three-day package offered by outfitters. Even so, a three-day total of 7696 doves would put this shooter ahead of the last record I heard for a one-day kill by a single man, and that was 2200-odd doves.

The lodge that placed the ad listed a web page, so I pulled it up. Among the other items on the page there was a list of names of the best 210 shooters who stayed at the lodge during the 2002 season. Also listed with the names were the number of shells fired and doves killed. The shooters travel to Argentina for eared doves during five months of the year. In approximately this time frame, the 210 shooters tallied 408,643 eared doves.

Keep in mind that this was just the kill from one outfitter. There are scores of others offering shooting in Argentina, Paraguay, and Uruguay. The combined kill of eared doves must reach unbelievable numbers, and it has been steadily increasing for the past decade or so.

By far, most of the eared dove shooting takes place in Argentina, at Cordoba, in a farming valley north of Buenos Aires. From 25 to 30 million eared doves are said to be in the Cordoba region. I was told that, as an ongoing attempt to relieve crop damage, the doves were sprayed on their roost with chemicals from planes and helicopters. In defense of the shooters who come to kill the doves, it is said that they are only killing a fraction of the population, are greatly aiding the farmers, bring much-needed American dollars into a depressed economy, provide needy people with protein in the form of dead doves, and are basically all-around good guys, friendly, outgoing, and there to see how things must have been with the passenger pigeon in North America. Sorry, but I strongly disagree. I have heard more than a few of these shooters laughingly say, "No one saved me any buffalo."

To me they are mindless shooters, with no interest in or respect for what they kill. I have felt this way for many years. During the time that Les Line was editor of *Audubon*, twenty or so years ago, I tried several times to get him to publish something about the South American shooting. I had hoped he would assign such an article to Ted Williams, who still writes very in-depth, highly personal articles for the magazine on controversial issues. Line wrote back that there were apparently a lot of doves down there. And that was that.

A couple of years ago I finally went to Argentina to see for myself. However, my principal interest was not eared doves, but rather picazuro and spot-winged pigeons. Several outfitters were advertising pigeon shooting along with the doves, and I was curious as to how they were holding up under the intense pressure. As it turned out, the pigeons were starting to show the signs of overshooting in the region where we were. We went at the time when a few ads started appearing in North American magazines suggesting shooters consider Paraguay and Uruguay rather than Argentina. I recall at least one ad for Uruguay stated: "Shooting like Argentina used to have."

We didn't shoot at Cordoba, but to the north, not far from Paraguay. I was told that it wasn't a region with high eared dove numbers, but there would be some dove shooting along with the pigeons. My wife and I were placed in a party of three others who we didn't know. Two of these were noted international bird shooters and at one time had been high officials in Ducks Unlimited.

The pigeons were there in good numbers, primarily the picazuro. During several mornings the shooting could be called steady. But the outfitter, in answer to my questions, confided that the numbers were dropping, and he was concerned about providing the numbers shooters expected in the coming years. The birds we encountered seemed wary, frequently flying high, and many of the shots were near the maximum range.

I had come to Argentina with the firm resolve to limit my kill, regardless of the number of birds encountered. For pigeons I felt fifteen per day would be my stopping point. For doves I planned a personal limit of twenty-five to thirty per day, which was roughly twice that of the limit for mourning doves in North America. I shot my personal limit of pigeons rather quickly. My wife took the gun and shot a few herself. Then we sat and watched the

mourning and white-winged doves (*Zenaida macroura* and *Zenaida asiatica*)

other shooters. I think they ended up with about sixty to ninety each, maybe more.

Because of the range involved, the shooters were certainly "dusting," "sailing," "hitting," "crippling," and "winging," many pigeons that didn't fall to earth after being shot. The number became apparent two days later when we passed the field and it was full of caracaras and vultures feeding on the pigeons not picked up by the bird boys assigned to each shooter.

Those who shoot pigeons have long known that they "take some killing" compared to other game birds. While a single pellet will cause a ruffed grouse to fall from the air, pigeons absorb hard hits and continue on. One only needs to look back into the records of various homing pigeons used during World War I and II to find the strength of these birds.

The most famous bird during World War I, Cher Ami, saved an entire American battalion. Once released, the pigeon flew a gauntlet of German bullets and shells. Shrapnel tore off one leg and passed through the breast. The other leg, on which the message was placed, hung by shreds of sinew. Yet the pigeon flew forty kilometers in twenty-five minutes. The mounted body of Cher Ami is in the Smithsonian today.

As Marge and I watched the other pigeon shooters, I mentioned that things were getting ugly. It was plain to see that many pigeons were duplicating Cher Ami's will to escape. The eared dove shooting bordered on being absurd. We shot in a two-hundred-acre milo field, in which I estimated there were around 20,000 to 25,000 doves. At sunrise they approached the field in a nearly unbroken dark cloud from their forest roost. The shooting went on from about 9:00 until 11:00 a.m. In that entire period there wasn't a span of five seconds without doves passing. The three other shooters shot upward of 500 each. To me it was mindless killing without justification, and it pointed to the disturbing truth in some of what Dallas Lore Sharp had expressed in 1914.

About the time I had the money to travel well beyond my home territory to hunt, I read an article in *Field & Stream* about white-crowned pigeon shooting in the Caribbean. I recall not fully understanding how the shooting was being done. It took place out in open water from a boat. The author mentioned that they had to race sharks to the downed birds.

All of this became much clearer in 1971 when Virginia Kraft wrote a superb and deeply disturbing article for *Sports Illustrated* entitled "Black Future for the White-Crown." She hit on the

white-crowned pigeon (*Patagioenas leucocephala*)

point surrounding the mass killing of pigeons and doves that I find so remarkably unacceptable and puzzling:

> If pigeons were as big as polar bears or as glamorous as leopards, there would be considerable growling among the watchdogs of the world's wildlife over the slaughter of the white-crowned pigeon. But the plight of *Columba leucocephala* [sic] has failed to arouse even a sympathetic sniff from those who should be concerned about its extinction. The signals are classic: the bird's nesting, breeding and feeding grounds are disappearing at an alarming rate, while widespread and indiscriminate killing continues unchecked. That such signals have not served as red alerts in this era of conservation awareness, if not to ornithologists certainly to sportsmen, is as mystifying as some of the bird's habits.

In Kraft's article I found the reason most of the shooting of white-crowned pigeons was done from a boat: The shooters were just offshore from the pigeon's breeding colonies and were killing the adults leaving to feed. Because, like the passenger pigeon, the whitecrown formed dense colonies, the best shooting took place during the breeding season.

Once while hunting sharptail grouse in Montana with Patrick Hemingway, I asked him about the whitecrowns in Cuba, and if his father ever shot them.

"Yes," he replied. "Frequently. That was a bloody affair, I can assure you," he added.

According to Kraft, hotels in the Bahamas had launched a campaign in the southern states to bring shooters in for pigeons. Apparently they came. Examples given by Kraft ranged from 150 Floridians who chartered two planes for a weekend shoot and killed more than 2500 pigeons to vast piles of birds "rotting and decaying where they had been abandoned, victims of irresponsible hunters."

Certainly the most disturbing part of Kraft's article was her investigation into the shooting taking place around Saona Island in the Dominican Republic. The island, forty square miles of uninhabited mangrove swamp, was the last major white-crowned pigeon nesting colony. At the time of her article the other two were in the Bahamas and lower Florida Keys, numbering about 10,000 pairs in each, while the Saona Island colony numbered 300,000.

Raul Villaverde, a local who knew the pigeons well, told Kraft that on weekends during the breeding season upward of fifty shooters averaged 7500 birds per day that were picked up. He estimated another 25 percent on top of that number were crippled and not recovered. The total is, of course, further compounded by the squabs in the nest that starved when the adults were killed. At the time of Kraft's article, Villaverde estimated that at least 100,000 whitecrowns had been killed around Saona in just a few years of shooting.

Apparently the shooters continued until the vast colony was all but wiped out. Mr. Simon Guerrero of the Dominican Republic's Parque Zoologico Nacional wrote me regarding this recently: "The Saona white-crowned pigeon colony was really a big one [a] long time ago. I don't think it is totally gone but very reduced. I have visited the island this past September 2003 and saw 20 birds flying from the mainland to Saona. According to local people there are still some incidents with illegal hunters."

Indeed, they are still shooting whitecrowns today. In the July/August 1999 issue of *Shooting Sportsman* there is an ad for whitecrown shooting in Cuba. It pictures an elderly shooter festooned with dead pigeons. Actually, there seems to be no end to the wholesale slaughter of pigeons and doves around the world, past or present.

Certainly one of the most striking of all the world's pigeons is the large New Zealand pigeon. It was used to illustrate the dust jacket of the reprint of Sir Walter Lawry Buller's *A History of the Birds of New Zealand* (1873), retitled *Buller's Birds of New Zealand* (1967). Buller wrote of the vast killings of the pigeons, as

white-winged dove (*Zenaida asiatica*)

more Europeans settled the two islands. In 1869 he wrote of a "sporting gentleman" who shot eighty-five in two mornings in a taraire grove at Ramarama. He noted that native Maoris took a great number for food: "In July and August 1882, Rawiri Kahia and his people snared no less than eight thousand of them in a single strip of miro brush at Opawa, near Lake Taupo." However, the New Zealand pigeon, unlike many of his kin, was offered aid early on. In 1896 a special act was passed to provide some protection. In 1921, as the result of the Animal Protection and Game Act, the pigeon gained total protection.

Another North American colony nester, the white-winged dove of the southwestern United States, Mexico, and Central America, was shot extensively in both Arizona and Texas until the early 1960s. The dove's population in the 1800s is estimated to have been in the many millions, with the largest concentrations being in Arizona along the Gila, Salt, and Santa Cruz Rivers.

The dove was first market hunted in the 1800s and early 1900s, then began attracting sport shooters. In the years after World War II, Arizona was the place to be for whitewing shooting. During some years the doves migrated early in September, so the shooters asked for and got an August season. It opened while the adults were still feeding young in the nest.

The Hollywood crowd adopted the Arizona dove shoot, with stars such as Clark Gable, Robert Taylor, and Andy Devine being regulars. A brewery and two firearms companies chartered planes to fly shooters in. There was a lot of gunfire and a lot of dead doves. The limit was twenty-five white-winged doves per day, but scant attention was paid to it. As one retired Arizona biologist told me, "No one seemed to want to step up and write Clark Gable a ticket for too many doves." Even though the State of Arizona did make some large-scale arrests for overshooting, it didn't stem the prevailing attitude of "If it flies, it dies."

It all came to a sudden halt in the early 1970s. Today Arizona's whitewing population is 90 percent smaller than it was in the 1960s. While the shooting was intense beyond reason, it was not the major factor for the dove's nearly overnight decline. It was brought about by the clearing of the mesquite thickets along the rivers for farmland starting in the 1950s. The doves nested in the mesquite, frequently a hundred pairs to the acre. Then the grain crops of the 1950s and 1960s were replaced with cotton. That amounted to the final death knell for the Arizona doves, and the shooters moved south into Mexico, where large populations could be found.

In the British Isles it was the large wood pigeon that was sought. On January 10, 1962, Major Archie Coats shot 550—one pigeon every 28.5 seconds. He wrote a book about his wood pigeon shooting in 1963 and set off a legion of followers to the point that wood pigeon shooting clubs were formed. No one has broken Coats's single-day record, but the desired daily bag is one hundred.

As mentioned, on the Pacific Coast, the bandtail had been removed from the protected list in 1932. Even after the 1911-12 overkill, the bird's real troubles were just beginning.

Wild Pigeon Shooting

Unfortunately, the bandtail is not a bird which can be managed, as
we say, by wildlife biologists even to the extent that the mourning
dove can. We can assist him indirectly by practicing intelligent
forestry, and by hanging on to those wilderness areas still left in the
West. Aside from that, our only management possibility is by discipline of our guns.

BYRON DALRYMPLE 1949

On December 1, 1932, the band-tailed pigeon was returned to
the legal list of game birds. Johnson Neff (1947) recalled the outcome, both in 1932 and in 1934, in an area where the birds had
gathered due to a heavy acorn fall:

> In winter, California is largely responsible for the fate of
> the bulk of the present band-tailed pigeon population
> of the Pacific Coast. In the Santa Lucia range of Monterey
> County, California, in the Monterey division of the Los
> Padres National Forest, there was, on December 1, 1932, a
> heavy wintering population of pigeons. The road leading
> to Tassajara Hot Springs resort, at a place close to 5000
> feet elevation, crosses a narrow saddle locally called China
> Camp, which separates two deep canyons, Miller and Calaboose. Oak and pine trees are abundant on the slopes near
> the summit of the mountains, and a short distance north
> of the saddle several wide and fairly open oak flats occur.

On the first day of the 1932 open season countless pigeons flew across China Camp saddle from Miller to Calaboose Canyons and back again. Certain hunters told the writer of watching gunners who shot all day long, assisting others to obtain their limits, and left piles of birds on the ground.

In 1934 there was again an ample food supply in the area adjacent to China Camp saddle, and a large flight of pigeons gathered there and in the adjacent flats known as Chews Ridge and White Oak Flat. On December 9 (Sunday) the writer again went to the shooting area. The entire mountain abounded with hunters, automobiles, and guns. Gunners covered every opening in the forest and shots poured into the pigeon flight from all directions and elevations. At China Camp saddle the picture was not pleasant, as ten men shot where one would have been enough. Sportsmanship was virtually absent. In the continued fusillade of long-range shots, many wounded pigeons plunged to earth or fluttered down to alight in shrubbery or trees. Owing to the steepness of the slopes and their dense vegetation, the loss of birds was very high, possibly as many as five pigeons being lost or mortally wounded for every bird picked up by a hunter.

Welcome back to the gun, *Patagioenas fasciata monilis.*

As Neff's reports about the early 1930s indicate, the band-tailed pigeon received the same treatment and attitudes as it had until the 1913 closed season. But this time the situation was more severe and continued to grow worse as the decades passed. The reason was the swelling in numbers of shooters and a much greater awareness that a wild pigeon was available for sport. There was a very small outcry from just a handful of individuals about the number of pigeons being killed after the season reopened. In 1934, due to the season dates in both Washington and Oregon, there were likely no legally killed bandtails in either state. In California the estimate was 51,056 pigeons killed. According to the few who had a concern about the pigeon, this figure was unacceptably high. Forty years later, in 1972, the Oregon and Washington kill was 250,000 and the California kill 500,000. This made what some call the "bad old days" of shooting look tame compared with modern times.

Much of the responsibility for calling hunters' attention to the bandtail can be traced back to the various state fish and game departments. For example, Oregon's Game Commission (today the former Fish Commission and Game Commission are joined as the Oregon Department of Fish and Wildlife) printed up a list of mineral springs and seashore sites as an aid to shooters. They also spread the word about the excellent pigeon shooting that could be found at such locations.

Many of the mineral springs and seashore sites in the Northwest had been known for attracting pigeons nearly since the first white settlers arrived. However, as the elderly individuals I questioned thirty and forty years ago pointed out, the sites were well known to locals, but not many "outsiders" knew of them. I was curious to learn how many people shot the sites prior to 1913 and then afterward during the first years of the reopened season.

Wes Batterson told me of one of the more graphic discoveries of a bandtail mineral site by outside shooters. Nehalem Bay, on the northern Oregon coast, supports one of the largest concentrations of pigeons in coastal Oregon. The birds stage in the mornings in the tall firs and spruce on the north end of the bay and come down to drink from pools in a maze of driftwood and logs. I've spent many dawns crouched behind weathered old logs watching and photographing the Nehalem pigeons. Of the coastal areas, it is by far my favorite.

According to Wes, a few locals shot pigeons there prior to the 1913 closure; after the season reopened they tried again but without success. This was due to an almost uniform lack of understanding or knowledge—in some cases, interest—regarding the bandtail by employees of most Northwest state game departments. When the season was reopened in 1932, Oregon and Washington set the dates as October 16–30.

I guess such a season could be termed comical if there wasn't total ignorance involved. On October 16 it would be very difficult to find a single band-tailed pigeon anywhere in Oregon or Washington. All but a few stragglers would have left the states three or four weeks previously. In Oregon, this season was in effect during the years of 1932–1938. For certain, bandtails in Oregon had nothing to fear from legal shooters during that time frame. In Washington, someone must have known something about pigeons. In 1935 the season was changed to open on September 16, and Washington shooters began killing some pigeons.

Wes Batterson was hired by Oregon's Game Commission on a temporary basis in 1934. Two years later he took a job on the Malheur National Wildlife Refuge near Burns, Oregon. In 1941 he was again hired by the Oregon Game Commission as a wildlife biologist for the northern Oregon coast. During much of the early stage of his career he had many dealings with Frank Wire, the Oregon market hunter during the 1890s and early 1900s and later long-time Oregon State Game Supervisor. Wes recalled telling Wire that Nehalem Bay had many bandtails, but the season was "all wrong for shooting them." As a result, in 1939 Oregon's bandtail season was opened on September 1. Washington soon followed suit, as did British Columbia. It was the start of an ugly chapter in North American bird shooting.

Wes told me that on that first September 1 opening, Frank Wire and friends from Portland came to Nehalem in numbers.

From that point on the groups of shooters swelled as the word spread. Within a few years opening day at Nehalem saw shooters nearly shoulder to shoulder.

World War II did much to halt bandtail shooting. Shotgun shells became difficult to obtain, gas was rationed, and men went off to war. However, certainly not all of them, it appears. Art Einarsen wrote of a mineral spring known as Pigeon Butte, south of Corvallis, Oregon, as it was in 1942. Today this spring is part of the William L. Finley National Wildlife Refuge. Einarsen's account appears in Neff's report of 1947:

> For years this pass has been popular with hunters. Because of the terrain and the usual eagerness of the hunter, most of the shots are at long distances, which result in a crippling loss averaging more than 60 percent of the pigeons bagged. When the number of birds killed (at each pass) is more than 600, as in 1942 at this pass, the seriousness of the slaughter can be recognized.
>
> The band-tailed pigeon will never have wide abundance. It is hunted on uneven ground, where a high percentage of crippled birds are lost and little effort is made to recover them. Five months after the season it was still possible to pick up birds which had died of injuries in large numbers around Pigeon Butte.

In Oregon, as elsewhere in the Northwest, the decade and a half after World War II was a sportsman's and wildlife biologist's dream. It really couldn't have been much better. With ample water in the Canadian prairie, waterfowl numbers went off the charts. Lakes and rivers teemed with trout. Large runs of salmon, steelhead, and sea-run cutthroats were commonplace. In the high desert regions mule deer were numerous. In the Willamette Valley ring-necked pheasants were everywhere, even inside the city

David Hagenbaumer
2003

limits of the capital of Salem. Mourning doves were exceedingly common. Compared to today, bandtail flocks could be termed "strong." Oregon was a large state, with a small population for its size. To a large degree, there was no need for wildlife biologists to manage. Everything shootable or catchable was doing just fine on its own.

By the 1970s much of this idyllic sportsman's wonderland was changing. The decline, slow at first, picked up momentum at a dizzying rate. As for the species that were hunted, all experienced their drastic decline not because of overshooting, but because of changes in agriculture and habitat loss. All, that is, except the band-tailed pigeon, which was shot down in ever-increasing numbers.

With a September 1 open season, most pigeon shooters took advantage of mineral springs and seashore sites. At such locations they had a bird that was captive to its needs. Even after being shot at, the pigeons would return again and again. Very simply, the birds required a drink of the special water. Starting in the late 1940s and early 1950s shooters began buying or leasing mineral sites for the pigeon shooting. In Oregon, Pigeon Butte, Kesters, Chesire, Nestucca, and Panther Creek were made into clubs. Crawfordsville, Aurora, and Whittakers were fee areas, with the landowners charging $1.00 to $2.50 for a day of pigeon shooting.

Of all the many mineral and seashore sites I have visited, the Crawfordsville spring strikes me as the most important, both from its long history and the number of pigeons that use it. For an inland mineral spring, it has likely attracted the largest number of band-tails of any in the Northwest. That fact is somewhat odd, because the majority of pigeons breed in the Coast Range or its foothills.

The Crawfordsville spring is located on the east side of the Willamette Valley, in the foothills of the Cascade Mountains. The spring itself is at the base of a timbered slope, across the

Calapooia River from the one gas station and store of Craw-fordsville, and upstream from the historical town of Brownsville. Like most mineral springs, it isn't much to look at. In fact, in late August and early September it takes some looking to find. About all that marks the spring are a few small pools of dirty, rusty, warm water. Frankly, it appears like a leak from a septic tank. But how the pigeons are attracted to it!

I recall talking with an elderly person in the region who told me the Kalapuya Indians trapped bandtails at the spring. I have little doubt that this was true, as there was once a strong group of Kalapuya, the Tsankapi band, in the region. The often-photo-graphed and interviewed Eliza was one of the last pure-blooded Kalapuya and lived at Brownsville until her death in 1922.

There are written accounts of market hunting at the spring, the birds being sent to Albany, Oregon, by wagon, and then on to Portland by train. Sport shooting followed that. By the 1940s the Crawfordsville spring was widely known in the region. The landowner at the time, R. Carter, charged $1.00 per day to shoot there. In 1946 Art Einarsen and Francis P. Schneider, who was then a district biologist for the Willamette Valley, Oregon Game Commission, made a report of the shooting at Crawfordsville. Schneider went on to head the Game Commission and was pre-sent during several of my first testimonies on behalf of the band-tail to the Oregon Fish and Wildlife Commissioners.

Art Einarsen was as much a hunter as he was a naturalist. But he had quickly joined a growing number of individuals who were trying to point out that the band-tailed pigeon was being man-aged poorly, and the bird wouldn't hold up under the shooting pressure it was being subjected to. Einarsen's 1946 report should have served as a wake-up call to a bad situation. But it certainly didn't. The only thing that came of Einarsen's report was that the limit was reduced from ten pigeons a day to eight.

Einarsen made this important observation: "The only redeeming fact is that people are not generally aware of the habitual roosts of these birds and when they learn that as many as ten thousand pigeons may come down in one day's flighting to a watering spot, a pigeon derby will be enacted that will be the shame of this age." Only a few years after Einarsen wrote this, the Oregon Game Commission made efforts to inform as many shooters as possible about pigeons and mineral sites. One has to wonder what Einarsen felt as a result.

Art Einarsen will go into history as being one of the very strong voices, among the few, that pointed out where the pigeon was headed. As for his first visit to Crawfordsville, he reported:

> Hunting was more intensive in the Oregon area than in any previous year. It was being promoted by sporting goods houses, who have learned of this early season outlet for arms and ammunition and have a more general knowledge of the hunting grounds where concentrations exist. The result is that gunners come in tens, yes, hundreds, to these favored spots and a remnant species again faces extermination.
>
> The band-tailed pigeon is not to be credited with the same staying powers that the waterfowl possess. They do not exert the same instinct of self-preservation. They are intent on one purpose when making use of an area and fly into roosting or loafing areas in the face of heavy gunfire. Waterfowl would break and scatter under similar action. The bandtails face the gunfire, give up their toll while the remnant again reforms after a few simple aerial maneuvers of escape, and the remainder of the flock again passes over the huntsman. We can hardly dwell on the life history of the band-tailed pigeon but a quick look at the hunting practices of the present will surely aid us in determining that there is need for action.

Like Johnson Neff reporting on the California shooting in 1932 and 1934, Einarsen was soured on the average pigeon shooter by attitudes displayed toward the bird:

> An estimate of the amount of shooting that took place can be made from the number of empty shotgun shell cartons on the ground. Four hundred twenty-nine cartridge boxes in good condition, indicating recent usage, were enumerated on the ground. This does not account for shells in vests or pocket or the cartridge boxes discarded and not found by the observers. On this basis it is obvious that over 10,000 shells were used and this may be only a partial indication of the total number of shells fired. Bear in mind that this hunting took place on about 10 acres of ground as far as the intensive shooting was concerned. Nothing in the days of the passenger pigeon can compare with the amount of shot thrown into the air at this spot.
>
> In an area where the gunners are concentrated it is obvious that long shots will predominate. The novice, the eager gunner, the greedy, the selfish, take impossible and scratch shots in the hope they will bag the bird before it comes over some man directly in its path and range. The result is many wounded birds scaling down to drop at great distance and since they are not on the regular line of flight, the hunter feels he cannot leave and miss additional shots to track them down.
>
> Previous experience with bandtail hunters is convincing that fully as many birds are lost as are bagged. Were this the only loss it would be sorry enough, yet the hunters are becoming more and more inclined to waste birds that they have bagged. It was found in the Crawfordsville area this year that birds which were molting, especially the young of the year, were often left to rot where the hunter had his

blind, or where he parked his car. Dozens of birds were found scattered through the area and no account could be made of the limitless number scattered through the woodland near at hand. This is not only the story at Crawfordsville; it is the same at Pigeon Butte and Pigeon Springs in Benton County, at Pacific City in Tillamook County, at Jewel, Birkenfeld and Waterloo. It will be the same under the present arrangement wherever the pigeons are found to concentrate. If corrective measures are not applied soon, it will be better to invoke a complete closure, work out a management plan based on the life history of the bird and then begin to harvest anew on a strict and managed plan.

It is interesting that Einarsen reported that hunters threw away pigeons they shot. Johnson Neff had also reported this. Byron Dalrymple wrote on the subject, stating: "Anyone who has ever hunted bandtails to any great extent will tell you that a great many birds shot by the average hunter wind up in the garbage can." Both Neff and Dalrymple were writing about bandtails shot in California. Their winter diet of acorns can give the pigeons a markedly bitter taste. This can be overcome by first soaking the meat in salt water, but few did so.

The pigeons shot and thrown away in Oregon would have been on a berry diet, most likely cascara. This adds a good flavor to the flesh. But even with the added flavor, a bandtail is tough. Their strong flight capability greatly strengthens the breast muscles, thus making the bird a real fork-bender on the table. Also, when roasted, the meat dries out. Removal of the meat from the bone and preparing it in a potpie makes the bandtail among the best of all wild birds for table use, but few know this or go to the extra trouble it takes to prepare them in that manner. In the mid-1970s I met someone who liked pigeon potpie, and I felt that his stomach got in the way of his common sense. More about this later.

At the time, Einarsen wasn't the only one concerned about the band-tailed pigeon. A contemporary of Einarsen's in wildlife matters was William B. Morse. In 1949 he wrote an article on the life history of the bandtail for the *Oregon State Game Commission Bulletin*. He called for a reduction of the bag limit, a shortened season, closing special areas (mineral springs), a weekly limit, and educating hunters. In 1950 Morse prepared a paper on the plight of the pigeon for the annual conference of The Western Association of State Game and Fish Commissions. He stressed the need for two things: closing special areas (mineral springs) and "continuing public education about the need of management." In 1957 Morse was still trying. He wrote an article for the *American Forester* pointing out poor management of the pigeon. On the other side of the issue the Oregon Game Commission had drawn up a list of mineral sites, making this available to interested hunters.

On August 31, 1956, I knew nothing of Einarsen's and Morse's concerns. On that day my father, Kent Mathewson, and I drove in darkness east of Brownsville. We had one of the Oregon Game Commission's lists of mineral springs and were attempting to find the Crawfordsville spring. Several weeks earlier my father had dropped by the Game Commission's office in Portland to inquire about hunting pigeons.

Our family had just moved from Martinsville, Virginia, to Salem that June. We were quickly coming to understand what a boggling wealth of game we had settled into the midst of. In terms of hunting and fishing, Oregon made Virginia seem very old and worn out. Dad spoke with someone in the Portland office who gave him the list of mineral springs. The man also drew a rough map to three or four, and that was what we were attempting to decipher.

After driving gravel roads for several hours, we gave up. It was nearly 11:00 p.m. He turned the car into a small logging drop yard and knocked on the door of a shack with a single light on inside. A woman answered the knock; according to Dad, she was very nervous about who we were and what we wanted. But she told him we were only a few miles from the spring. We must have passed it in order to get there, and in the morning we couldn't miss the place with all the cars and trucks that would be present. And, yes, we could park over by the logs for the night. We had a new '56 Chevy station wagon and climbed into sleeping bags for the night.

My father loved—and likely still does—those goopy, sticky, sweet rolls that come in a sheet of six or eight. The ones with the thick white icing and raisins in the rolls. He also liked canned orange juice. Dad has always been firm that he hates coffee, a shortcoming that I now think had a lot to do with his common morning irritability. At any rate, we woke just before dawn, and he opened the sweet rolls, along with a 46-ounce can of orange juice. Either, by itself, is perfectly fine. But together they clash. The extreme sweetness of the rolls and the tart, near bitterness of the old-style orange juice (it comes a lot sweeter today) met on the tongue to create an effect only slightly removed from biting into an unripe persimmon.

His standard hunting or fishing breakfast over, we set out to find the spring. As the woman had said, it wasn't difficult. Cars and trucks were passing steadily as we ate. We followed them off a gravel road and out into an open field. In 1956 the Crawfordsville spring was owned by the Jenks family, rather well known in that part of the Willamette Valley for their chicken hatchery.

Before entering, a fellow took $2.00 for each of us and wrote out a small, heavy paper card. I still have it, as I keep nearly everything. (As we get older, my wife is coming increasingly to the hand-wringing stage with worry about what she will do with it all when I am gone.) The old card reads: "This entitles bearer to hunt Pigeons on designated area, on this day only." It is signed and dated, and printed in smaller letters below is: "Management reserves the right to refuse or revoke admittance at anytime."

More than any other place I've been during those first days when summer turns to early fall, the *smell* in Oregon's Willamette Valley is strongest. It's spicy. And just before dawn it can be a damp sort of spicy, because of the morning's chill and the first dew of fall. Before the first of that smell, the summer is hot, everything still green and quiet under the weight of the heat. Nearly overnight the grasses turn brown, some leaves on trees start to show a little color, the grasshoppers and yellow jackets are at their height, and that smell of dawn is overpowering—and all pure Oregon. I have grown to love it as much as anything in the Northwest. I got my first real encounter with that smell about 6:00 a.m. on September 1, 1956.

When we parked, many other shooters were walking across a flat, grassy field to a timbered hillside. We crossed a ditch that was bone-dry. Dawn was coming fast, and Dad urged me to hurry up so that we could get a good spot. But up on the hillside all the spots, be they "good" or "not so," were taken, with more shooters arriving steadily. Sportsmanship firmly dictates that one never crowds another shooter who has arrived at a spot first. So Dad looked around confused as others walked up to stand very near us, and we were some of the first there. Then we understood. There was no consideration given to "spot" territory.

Just a little after dawn the first small flock of bandtails arrived. They surely came from a distance because when I first saw them they were faint dots in the sky. But they came fast, and once over the spring area they folded their wings and rushed down as only a bandtail can. The series of graceful twists and turns as they dropped was like a dance. They apparently wanted to settle in the tops of the conifers on the hillside, but they didn't have that chance. The entire area exploded in gunfire.

The shooting was nearly nonstop from more than a hundred shooters. It went on steadily for over an hour as flocks of pigeons swept overhead. The firepower was so concentrated that few birds survived it. Cheers and yells and laughter rang out after flocks were shot down.

It was impossible to know who shot what. I doubt that anyone actually killed a pigeon solely on his own; rather, falling birds were hit multiple times by several shooters. There was a lull, and then more pigeons began coming. I didn't know what this second wave was until years later—it was the flight of females following the males.

The limit in 1956 was eight bandtails per day. When we left at about noon, Dad and I had claimed thirteen pigeons between us. Seemingly everyone else had nearly as many.

I feverishly wish now I could say that the carnage caused me to never return to Crawfordsville or any other mineral spring. It didn't. I shot at Crawfordsville until the mid-1960s. After the first few years I always made it a point to go high on the ridge to get away from the crowd. This would work well in terms of having the shooting to myself. However, in most years I would fill my limit not from birds I bagged, but from crippled or dead pigeons I encountered while up there. Many bandtails were able to fly out of the killing zone, then flutter to the ground or die high on the ridge.

My last year at Crawfordsville was 1966. I met Gene Silovsky, who was working on his thesis, "Distribution and Mortality of the Pacific Coast Band-tailed Pigeon," at Oregon State University. What he was doing at the spring was asking shooters if he could cut open the pigeons' crop to see if they were actively producing pigeon milk. If so, this would indicate they were still feeding a squab when shooting season began.

He was only able to check a small number of the pigeons killed that day. Of seventy-four males checked, fifty-two had active or stimulated crops. Only twenty-two had normal crops, indicating they weren't feeding squabs. Of eighty-two females checked, forty-eight had active or stimulated crops, which left thirty-four as normal.

Art Einarsen had been on to this important insight fully twenty years previously. When checking pigeons shot during early September, he found that they had active crops. He wrote: "It was not until September 18 that all birds taken had glands inactive or receding in activity. Up to that time both males and females with active glands predominated. It is apparent, then, that these two clues point to a season which is too early when it falls on the first day of September in this range." Silovsky's thesis showed the same thing. When the shooting of bandtails began in British Columbia, Washington, and Oregon, many pigeons still were caring for a young in the nest. And of course, with the adults shot, it is inevitable that the squab starved.

Gene Silovsky's thesis was made public in June 1969. As is common practice, a copy of any work at Oregon State University on game birds, mammals, or fish is sent to the Oregon Department of Fish and Wildlife for their files and for biologists to use in their work. Silovsky's thesis went to the Oregon Game Commission. Like Einarsen's information regarding bandtails before it, it was ignored.

The Bandtail Question

Now comes the era of Modern Game Management with its scientific wisdom. And bandtails live happily ever after. Right? Wrong! While there may be elements of a fairy tale about this story, it definitely lacks a happy ending.

ROBERT JARVIS 1988

FOR ME, bandtails and the town of Valsetz were synonymous. And when I think about it, I would have liked Valsetz preserved in some manner. As for why or for what use, I come up short. But I do miss Valsetz. It was an important part of my life for more than thirty years. Down below the log pond, on past where the North Fork of the Siletz enters the mainstream Siletz River, I had a cascara ridge where I hunted bandtails. I like to think I was a hunter of the pigeons for all of those years, rather than a shooter. While the birds end up dead either way, there is an important difference.

Valsetz was built in the upper Siletz Valley, at a point where this well-known river can be jumped across. Far downstream, down where the Siletz slides into the Pacific, at tidewater, is the house constructed for the movie version of Ken Kesey's *Sometimes a Great Notion*, which starred Paul Newman.

Valsetz was a company town. Everything—the homes, the school, the store, the bowling alley, the café, the mill, the log pond—was owned down to the last nail by Cobbs & Mitchell initially, then Templeton Lumber Company, and finally Boise Cascade. The town was founded in 1919, and by 1920 it was granted a post office. The school came in 1929. When I first started going to Valsetz in the 1950s, close to 500 mill workers and loggers lived there. Their families swelled the population to nearly 1100. It amounted to a lot of people living far out in the timber, away from everyone else.

If you worked there, you rented a house from the company. You bought your food from the company store. You paid your phone and power bill to the company. Then everything was deducted from your paycheck. There were other company timber towns in the Northwest, but none as complete or isolated as Valsetz. Oregonians spoke of going "down into Valsetz" because it was most commonly reached by a sixteen-mile gravel road from Falls City to the east. Most of these miles are traveled by a steep, downward plunge into the Siletz Valley. On the western side of Valsetz there is a narrow road following the river down to the town of Siletz, but few used it, and during periods of high fire danger it was gated and locked just below the North Fork.

I have no idea how many times I went down into Valsetz over the years. But I do remember with clarity the time I made a misjudgment and took Pat Hemingway down there. He had flown into Portland after a week of Atlantic salmon fly-fishing in New Brunswick. I picked him up at the airport along with three salmon he had caught and frozen. It was after 9:00 p.m. when we collected his baggage and drove to my home in Salem.

Our plans for the next several days were to fish for steelhead and sea-run cutthroat in the Siletz River. We would use my camper van for sleeping. He was exceedingly tired from his travels, and wisdom should have dictated that we spend the night at my home and then depart the next morning. But I decided to leave after we put his salmon in my freezer so we could be fishing at dawn, an important time frame for summer steelhead. There are good paved roads the entire way to the section of river we would be fishing, and being late, there wouldn't be much traffic to contend with.

However, I decided to use the road from Falls City to Valsetz, then down the river route. It would shave off a few miles and give Pat an Oregon culture tour. One thing led to another and it was after 1:00 a.m. when we left. Pat was nodding by the time we reached Falls City but became wide awake as I started bouncing along the dusty, rutted, gravel road.

I was in a hurry to get to the place I wanted to fish so that he could get a little sleep, and I drove faster than normal. Some of the curves down into Valsetz are close to switchbacks, and for most of them Pat was ramrod straight and strangely quiet. He is usually very talkative. I suddenly understood my error. Falls City to Valsetz should only be driven in daylight the first time and only when a person is fully rested.

Valsetz had a unique flavor. Nine-year-old Dorothy Anne Hobson began publishing the *Valsetz Star* in 1937, doing so until 1941. The folksy newspaper became famous nationwide, with Mrs. Franklin D. Roosevelt once quoting from it during a press conference. Dorothy Anne wrote weekly gems such as: "We want our paper to stand for something, so we had a meeting, and we stand for kindness. Also, we are a Republican paper, but we will not charge democrats any more for a copy than Republicans." She always made a point of capitalizing *Republican* but not *democrat*. Regarding her stand for kindness, she received a letter from Shirley Temple.

In the 1970s and 1980s progressive Salem juvenile judge Albin Norblad used the Valsetz log pond to implement a firewood for the elderly program. Sunken logs were salvaged and work crews of youthful offenders from his court cut and split firewood, which was given free to the elderly on a fixed income. This program also gained national attention.

I loved Valsetz. I fished the log pond for cutthroat trout, always harboring the hope of catching one of the few brown trout also present. Those Valsetz browns likely were the westernmost population in North America, unless Vancouver Island's Cowitchan River is further west, as it likely is when I stop to think about it. Some of my best fly-fishing for summer steelhead took place near Valsetz. There are crawfish in the Siletz that reach the size of small lobsters, and I had several traps that I set each year.

The store at Valsetz, with the plank front porch, was a Northwest classic. It always was necessary to stop there for the all-time Oregon snack, a cold Dr. Pepper and several long sticks of pepperoni, or a full-blown lunch at the café. Their hamburger basket was fully logger tested. It wasn't of the wimpy status served by chains today with claims of being huge or colossal. A Valsetz café burger was as thick as a wedge of fir, and the basket was filled with most of a peck of spuds.

In 1984 Valsetz came to a sudden end. The big timber was gone, so Boise Cascade decided to close the mill and remove the town. The log pond was drained, the people moved out. Soon afterward bulldozers knocked everything down, and the debris was then burned. The next year Douglas firs were planted where the town once stood. They grew fast, and it is now as though Valsetz never existed.

Of all my Valsetz memories, none are stronger or more important than those of bandtails high on the ridges along the river below the town. To reach them I would drive through Valsetz in darkness and snake my way down river past the North Fork. There were no markers, just a place I remembered from year to year to park off to the side.

As it began to grow light I would pull myself up the steep

canyon slopes using vine maples and waist-high ferns as hand-holds as I climbed. About halfway up I entered the cascara grove. The trees reached all the way to the summit. On the top were stumps of the huge old growth Douglas fir, felled with crosscuts and moved with horses. Most were in their final stages of decay,

but several were intact enough that I could climb up and stand on them. Their width was that of a kitchen table or more.

I would find my lofting pole from previous seasons, attach the hand-carved cork and cedar bandtail decoys to it, and raise it above the cascara. Right after dawn the entire ridge would be alive with flocks of arriving pigeons. I never felt any guilt about shooting them, and due to my Lab, I never shot anything we didn't find. I never encountered another hunter there, even though the pigeons could number several hundred.

I left Oregon in 1971 for New Zealand, Australia, British Columbia, and Central America. When I returned to the ridges below Valsetz in 1974 very few pigeons were there. Nor were there many in any other place I looked. The flocks appeared to have vanished. In fact they had.

In 1972, while I was becoming increasingly interested in the New Zealand pigeon and spending time trying to photograph it in the mountains behind my rented cabin on the shores of Lake Taupo, the wintering bandtails in California gathered in the foothills on the west side of the Sacramento Valley. The attraction was an unusually heavy fall of acorns. It was exactly the circumstance as in 1911–1912, 1934, and to a lesser degree 1946. Once again, shooters surged into the region. The result was an estimated kill of 536,800 bandtails. Until that time the annual California kill was around 250,000. The 1972 kill in Oregon and Washington was also high, approaching 300,000.

Unlike many other game birds, waterfowl for example, state fish and wildlife departments have no knowledge of the actual number of bandtails. For years I made a habit of asking anyone who I felt might know. In all cases the answer was similar to the one James C. Bartonek, Pacific Flyway Representative, U.S. Fish and Wildlife Service, wrote to me in 1987: "Worth, sorry but no one in the FWS has the 'about' numbers for bandtails you want."

I did get some speculative figures from several people. They guessed that the total number of pigeons on the Pacific Coast was around a million to a million and a half prior to 1972. Using these estimates, and I think they are about right, the kill of 800,000 bandtails in 1972 amounted to half or more of the entire population. For certain, after the 1972 blasting, the timbered ridges, the brushy canyon walls, all the old bandtail haunts were nearly devoid of gray forms.

One method of obtaining an idea of the pigeon's numbers was by counting them in late August at mineral sites. The Oregon Game Commission began doing this at a few key mineral sites in 1961. At Crawfordsville the 1972 count was 487 pigeons. Of course, this count was made several months prior to the vast overkill in California. In 1975 there were 37 bandtails counted at Crawfordsville.

In the summer of 1974 I was back in Oregon from Central America. My interest in bandtails had grown considerably, and I began visiting mineral sites in Washington. I also met Mike Passmore, who was working on his thesis, "Utilization of Mineral Springs by Band-Tailed Pigeons." On August 3, I was invited to join Mike Passmore and his advisor, Dr. Robert Jarvis, at the Long Tom River mineral spring. They were cannon-netting pigeons to band and sex. At the time I had the opinion that bandtails should not be shot at mineral sites, my sole reason being that I felt it was unsporting. After spending time with Passmore and Jarvis at the Long Tom spring, the Nashville spring, and the Finley National Wildlife Refuge spring, I came to understand that more was going on by killing pigeons at such sites than just poor sportsmanship.

As the result of their work at mineral springs, Passmore and Jarvis discovered the males first/females second order of visits to the mineral sites. More important, they found a clearly marked age factor with birds at the springs. Nearly all the pigeons were older, mature birds. These, they speculated, were breeders that nested twice a season. (It has since been found that a very few pairs will breed three times.) Finally, they suspected that a good number of the birds encountered in late August were still feeding a squab in the nest. Since nearly all the pigeons at mineral sites were clearly older birds, Passmore and Jarvis determined that shooting bandtails at such sites had resulted in a slow, steady drain of breeding pairs capable of producing two squabs per year, rather than one. This, over time, was having an effect on the population.

Actually, prior to 1972 the band-tailed pigeon population was already showing signs of a decline. The mineral spring shooting, which had grown steadily since 1946, had been taking many pigeons. At Crawfordsville in 1949 there were more than 600 pigeons killed on September 1. Ten years later the opening day kill was generally in the 180–250 range. Other sites showed direct declines as well. Still others, such as West Monmouth and Salt Creek, were listed by the Oregon Game Commission as "shot out."

After the summer of 1974 I decided to try to secure some action by the Oregon Game Commission to halt shooting at mineral springs. To do this I drove up to Portland to talk with Chester Kebbe, who at that time was a staff biologist in Small Game Management. Everything dealing with game birds had to clear Kebbe's desk first.

This wasn't my first dealing with him. Six years previously, when I had become aware of the disappearance of peregrine falcons, especially the pairs along the Oregon coast, I had talked with him. Much of my concern regarding Oregon's peregrines was centered on the aging ornithologist Alex Walker. While not related to pigeons, the Alex Walker saga is worthwhile, therefore I include it here.

Alex Walker was a retired cheese-maker with a home in Pleasant Valley on the northern Oregon coast. In the nearby city of Tillamook the entire second floor of the Tillamook Historical Society Museum is devoted to his work. He had prepared numerous panoramas of Northwest species of birds and animals, plus trays of bird eggs he had collected.

Since he was a living member of ornithology's old school, I had spent a lot of time with Alex over several years in the late 1960s. He was painfully hard of hearing on his best days, some days being simply deaf. I learned to hand-write my questions to him ahead of time and carry a pad and pen for additional ones I might think of. I also had a card that read "Common name?" as he made a habit of discussing birds only in their Latin names. I used that card frequently.

If he was in the museum I had no problems with instant interviews. If he was in his tidy little home, difficulties arose. Alex was a widower, and he lived alone. He couldn't hear a knock on the door. On several occasions I needed to look in, see where he was, and run around outside the windows waving my arms to catch his attention. I learned the best location to do this was by the large bird feeder outside the kitchen window.

Alex got his first paying ornithological job in 1912 when William L. Finley hired him as a collector for the State of Oregon. Alex shot and skinned birds, while also collecting eggs. The rarer the bird, the more the skin or eggs were worth. Alex was very good as a collector. He went on to become one of the chief collectors for the Cleveland Museum of Natural History in Ohio.

Aside from collecting for museums and agencies, Alex, like all ornithological collectors, sold skins and eggs to other collectors. There were several magazines published for collectors, and bird eggs and skins were sold and traded as in the philatelic hobby. This grew to be such a problem that in the 1930s the Audubon

Society once stamped their name on Florida sandhill crane eggs in nests to make them worthless to collectors. While Alex spent his working life as a cheese-maker, he earned appreciable money from his collecting.

Although he ranged far and wide, Alex centered the vast majority of his efforts close to home. As a result, some of the more uncommon species suffered during his long years in the field. For example, a regional race of merlin, called the black pigeon hawk in Alex's time, became a specialty for him. This race of merlin is much darker than other races, as is the Peale's peregrine falcon, also of the Northwest coast. If there is a skin of a black merlin in a collection, odds are great that Alex was the one who shot it.

I had first called on Alex in the hope he could tell me the locations of the peregrine aeries along the coast so I could visit them to see if any breeding pairs remained. This posed no problem for him. With a map I had brought, he made numerous check marks up and down the coast. Then he walked over to a file cabinet, pulled out two large drawers, and showed me rows of peregrine skins. Another drawer held sets of eggs. He told me in detail which aerie the skins or eggs had been taken from. I left weak-kneed with the realization of just how many Oregon peregrines he had killed over the years.

Alex, certainly one of the major bird killers of all time in our region, was a dramatic example of the total lack of knowledge often displayed by those who oppose hunting. The National Audubon Society recognizes the important role that sport hunting plays in the large picture of wildlife management today. However, some local Audubon Society chapters don't agree. The Salem Chapter has long been riddled with very strong anti-hunting members. During a period when I attended many monthly meetings, they were held at the Morningside School in South Salem. Prior to the meeting, coffee, tea, and cookies were served.

The activity around the beverage table reminded me of a well-used feeder. People collected like a flock of evening grosbeaks. There was merriment, smiles, chatter, and total good will.

At one meeting I attended a government trapper was asked to give a program on his coyote control in eastern Oregon. When I arrived everybody was seated. The cookie tray appeared untouched. If anyone spoke, it was in a whisper. The overall feeling in the room was like a fog bank. The trapper gave a good presentation, even though he looked nervous during most of it. It was met with a polite smattering of claps. Then the meeting ended, as it had begun, quietly and noticeably reserved.

The very next month Alex Walker, with the aid of his son, gave a program. What a marked contrast! The chatter around the room was nearly a din. Smiles were broad, the room's mood upbeat. Little knots of people were approaching Alex, attempting to speak with him. They approached him as they would a major celebrity. And all seemed delighted they had been in his presence.

I sat in my chair, both in mild disbelief at what was transpiring in the room and feeling highly amused. I gleefully conjured up a wild fantasy about Alex leading this group on a birding trip to the coast and encountering a small flock of the remarkably beautiful black oystercatchers. In my fantasy, while the group scrambled for their field glasses for a better look, with a chorus of ohs and ahs, a few couldn't help but notice Alex's instant reaction.

"What are you doing with that gun, Mr. Walker?"

BLAM!

"Oh no, Mr. Walker!"

Just a month previously the group had been only barely tolerant of being in the same room with a man who trapped coyotes in an attempt to protect antelope fawns, and now they were cooing around a man who had likely killed more species of birds than they had on their life lists.

My first trip to Portland to speak with Chet Kebbe was the result of viewing Alex's peregrine skin and egg collection. At the time Alex still held a federal collecting permit that allowed him to kill just about anything he encountered. I asked Kebbe if it wasn't far past time that someone, like himself, consider getting the permit revoked. He said he would look into it.

During my 1974 meeting with Kebbe on bandtails and mineral springs, he listened but didn't offer much in reply. He did point out that pigeon shooting was important, because it was the first season to open, and that a lot of shooters liked to shoot at mineral springs. I left feeling I had accomplished little, if anything.

In 1975 Bob Jarvis suggested I give public testimony to the commissioners of the newly formed Oregon Fish and Wildlife Commission. The former Fish Commission and Game Commission had been joined, with John McKean appointed director. There were seven commissioners appointed by the governor: Louisa Bateman, Allan Kelly, John Boyer, Walter Lofgren, Frank Pozzi, McKee Smith, and Jack Steiwer. Bob Jarvis had drawn up some concerns about shooting pigeons at mineral springs and had sent them up to Chet Kebbe to pass along to the commissioners.

My intent was to state that shooting bandtails at mineral springs was unsporting because the birds were literally trapped due to their need for sodium water. Sportsmen don't practice methods other than fair chase. I was also planning to mention the concerns of Jarvis and Passmore regarding the drain on breeding pairs because of mineral site shooting. I had never given testimony before, so Bob offered me some coaching. There would be a lot of individuals giving testimony on a wide range of subjects, so he suggested that I keep mine short and to the point. Also he said that Louisa Bateman was the most progressive member on the commission, so I should direct my presentation to her.

Three things happened with my testimony in 1975. Louisa

showed the most interest, but was puzzled when I said that Dr. Jarvis had sent up bandtail information for them. She hadn't seen anything of that nature. John Boyer questioned why a halt of mineral spring shooting was justified, as in his words, "That is the only place you can hunt them." (I found out later that his concern was based on the fact that he was a member of the club that owned and shot the Cheshire spring.) Allan Kelly reminded me that the Oregon Fish and Wildlife Commission didn't legislate sportsmanship. If that was my major concern, the commission wasn't in the position to address it. Such a matter was best left to sportsman's clubs.

I was disappointed in my results. And afterward, I questioned Kebbe about what Jarvis had sent him to give to the commissioners. He brushed it off, saying he didn't feel the information was important, so he didn't give it to them.

The year 1975 was a difficult time for those in the various divisions of the Oregon Department of Fish and Wildlife. The situation with huntable and catchable species was beginning to change rapidly for the worse. The department is very much a business, unlike other state agencies. It depends on revenue from sales of hunting and fishing licenses for income. Its business is to produce wildlife for profit.

State wildlife biologists are under continuous pressure. Legislators criticize nearly everything they do, and citizens who hunt and fish demand more game or fish. Both of Oregon's game and fish departments had long operated in the promote-from-within method. One moved up through the ranks, having started as a fence-post-pounding field biologist. It was a good old boy system, headed by the best of the good olds. More important, during the mid-1970s, those in charge had worked nearly their entire careers when life was easy because Oregon was jam packed with nearly everything that ran, flew, jumped, or swam. But suddenly the skies, forest, and streams were becoming empty, and it wasn't a situation they were prepared to face. The fact that wild pigeons were thought by a few people to be adversely affected by shooting at mineral springs was very near the bottom of their concerns. Mule deer herds and salmon stock were declining, and those two were the chief moneymakers in license sales. Pigeons? Maybe later.

In 1976 I was heartened somewhat. For the first time the department had recruited from the outside, rather than promote from within—and the individual held a Ph.D. to boot! Dr. John Donaldson replaced John McKean as director. In addition, Herb Lundy replaced McKee Smith as a commissioner. Lundy was the editorial page editor for Portland's *Oregonian*, the largest newspaper in the state. I felt that these two men would aid me in acting on the bandtail problem. They were, to put it bluntly, better educated than the average person connected with the department or commission.

It proved to be wishful thinking. I came to the 1976 commission hearing with copies of Dr. Jarvis's suggestions about mineral spring shooting. I handed them out myself. As previously, I asked that action be taken to do away with shooting bandtails at mineral sites. I again stressed poor sportsmanship and the harm done to the pigeon's population by such shooting. I also gave my personal opinion of the lowering of pigeon numbers. I asked the commission to direct the department staff to first print an article in the department's monthly *Oregon Wildlife* to explain the problems caused by killing pigeons at mineral sites. This would aid in making shooters aware of the problem, as next to none had any idea why the pigeons came into these sites. After this public education, the next step I suggested would be to close the mineral sites to shooting.

Louisa Bateman was instantly interested in the public education first step. She instructed Ralph Denney, who was to replace the retiring Chet Kebbe, to see that such an article was written and published. He went on record as saying it would be done.

As for closing mineral springs to shooting, both John Boyer and Herb Lundy had strong opinions. Once again Boyer made the point that the only place to shoot bandtails was mineral springs. So if you took that away, nothing was left. I countered by saying that I hunted them far from mineral sites, in feeding locations with decoys, and that a sportsman didn't need to hunt mineral sites. At that point Allan Kelly reminded me, as he had done in 1975, that the commission didn't legislate sportsmanship.

But it was Herb Lundy's two remarks that stopped me cold. I had placed more than a little hope on gaining his support, although I had never seen him prior to that time. He was very much an intelligent looking person. When I first began my testimony, I was encouraged that he became alert. Several other members looked very bored; one even looked like he was going to drop off into a doze. Lundy listened carefully to everything I said, and waited until Bateman, Boyer, and Kelly had finished. Then he spoke.

Slowly, but with force, he looked me straight in the eye and said, "I like pigeon potpie." He paused, perhaps to let the words sink in, and then smiled broadly at everyone in the room and the other commissioners. To me, the entire five-word speech was very much like the scene from "The Graduate" when Mr. McGuire utters the one word to Benjamin Braddock: "Plastic." The firmness of his delivery made me feel suddenly foolish, as if I were wasting these people's time with an unimportant subject. After all, here is a man who writes some of the most important editorials in the state. I sputtered something to the effect that I too liked pigeon potpie.

He nodded and then addressed the other commissioners, not

me. He told them that his shooting buddy and he were attempting to make their own mineral spring by using rock salt in a clear water seep. He said he got the idea from Wes Batterson who had made one on the state's elk refuge in the Coast Range. Apparently pigeons had started to use it. He said that if he and his buddy were successful in their project, they would have their own private place to shoot pigeons. John Boyer smiled broadly at that remark.

Regarding this 1976 effort, I made next to no impression on the commissioners aside from Louisa's interest in shooters' education via a bandtail article. But after I finished speaking, Ralph Denney stopped me in the hall and told me the limit on pigeons was going to be cut from eight to five per day. He felt that would go a long way toward curtailing the drain in the population.

In 1977 I took a slide presentation to show the commissioners. No article had been published in *Oregon Wildlife* for shooter's education about bandtails. Louisa Bateman's term had expired, and she was no longer on the commission. After showing 35-mm transparencies of the pigeon's life cycle from egg to adult, I again asked for shooter's education and a ban on mineral spring shooting. The commissioners thanked me for the nice program and moved on to other subjects.

Ralph Denney, on the other hand, had something to say about my call for a ban on mineral site shooting. He disagreed with such an idea. Out in the hall he told me that there was no difference between shooting pigeons at mineral sites and shooting waterfowl at clubs where corn was planted and flooded. I countered with something to the effect that there was a large difference. After being shot at, waterfowl tend to become wary and will find other places to feed. The pigeons just keep coming back because they have no other choice. Also I asked him pointedly where was the article Louisa Bateman had instructed him to have written and published. He told me he hadn't gotten around to it yet, in a tone that clearly showed he had little or no interest in the idea. It was at that point I had every reason to believe that Ralph Denney had developed a dislike for me. I certainly had grown to dislike him. We were on equal ground.

After 1977 I switched my tactics. Because it is a migratory bird, the band-tailed pigeon comes under the direct control of the federal government. Other game birds, such as quail, grouse, and pheasants, are solely under the control of the state's agencies. But with migratory birds, the State of Oregon is required to follow the U.S. Fish and Wildlife Service's directives. With waterfowl, the federal control is extremely hands-on, so much so that frequently there is no love lost between state wildlife biologists and those working for the federal government. As for pigeons and doves, however, it seems that the U.S. Fish and Wildlife Service's control was much less. It appeared to me that they let the state do pretty much as they wished.

I began making visits to the Portland office of the U.S. Fish and Wildlife Service. I strongly suggested that Oregon's Department of Fish and Wildlife was doing a miserable job of managing the band-tailed pigeon and that the federal people should step in to dramatically alter this. After all, I pointed out, the band-tailed pigeon was "their bird." I never felt that anything I said made any difference.

Ralph Denney's reduction of the limit from eight to five birds, which he felt certain would solve the problem of the decreasing number of pigeons, proved unsuccessful. Bob Jarvis continued to call for cessation of the killing of mature breeders and gained some support. He then came up with a way around needing to ban mineral spring shooting. He and Mike Passmore had found that by mid-September many pigeons ceased visiting mineral sites and were preparing for migration. He suggested that the opening day of shooting be moved to a date several weeks later than the old established September 1. In 1980 this was done. The opening day was set for September 13.

While I felt this was an extremely important move in the right direction, I was still angry with Ralph Denney and his staff for failing to address the real problem—the killing of any pigeon at such mineral sites, be it on September 1 or September 30. Also it was apparent that they weren't going to clue pigeon shooters in as to what was going on at mineral sites. By that time I had written articles for *Gray's Sporting Journal, Field & Stream, Outdoor Life*, and *Sporting Classics* on bandtails. I mentioned in each article the negative effect shooting at mineral sites had on the bird. But all was hush from those in actual control in Oregon.

This step-in-the-right-direction season was short lived. In 1982 Ralph Denney returned the opening day to September 1. When I asked him why, he was brief and to the point: "It was very unpopular with pigeon shooters." What he left unsaid was the basic underlying fact concerning the Oregon Department of Fish and Wildlife: unless the general taxpayers step up and fund the department, they are in the business of selling hunting and fishing licenses. And a businessman's first rule is to keep the customer happy.

By 1987 the band-tailed pigeon numbers were in even more serious decline. I had resumed my attempts with the commission, asking for the return to the delayed season, to be followed by a ban on all mineral site shooting. My chief argument was that there was no need to shoot pigeons at mineral sites. I no longer had to worry about John Boyer as a commissioner and his membership in a mineral spring shooting club. His term was up and he went on to be investigated for several suspected game violations by the Oregon State Police. Then he left the state.

I think I was mostly correct about hunting bandtails away from mineral sites not unduly affecting the population, although most shooters wouldn't go to the effort required to hunt pigeons in their frequently difficult to reach feeding areas. At that time, though, I had not understood what was going on at several "pigeon passes" that had been shot heavily for years. To a degree these passes were nearly as bad as the mineral spring shooting.

Today I have a better understanding of these passes. Most are in Oregon's Coast Range, and they represent natural gaps that pigeons use daily while feeding. Most are high on ridges, and most have very heavy vegetation surrounding them. The shooters crowd into these gaps in the mountains and shoot as the pigeons pass. Long-range shooting is the norm, and the crippling rate is worse than one's worst nightmare. Some, such as the Alsea Pass, saw upward of fifty hunters a morning in the firing line.

Ron Saylor, a retired Alaskan tugboat man and locally famous carver of duck decoys at Florence, Oregon, recently wrote me about a popular pigeon pass in his part of the coast:

> This letter is in regard to our conversation we had on the phone about the pigeons not being recovered. The area I was telling you about was the south bank of the Siuslaw River, about 4 miles up Sweet Creek Rd. turning right on Burnhart Rd. then on to Duncan Island Bridge. The most shooting took place about 1.5 miles before the bridge and about 1.5 miles past the bridge. This would be about where the power lines cross Duncan Island and the river.
>
> The spot at the base of the power line tower is where I was able to smell the unretrieved birds. I only hunted there a couple of times because it was much too hard to retrieve the birds. This was about 1973.
>
> Later I became friends with Jim Mohr and during a conversation with him, he mentioned he had been at the power line area and had also smelled the rotten birds. This

was in 1965. He also told me he had known two brothers that had hunted pigeons a lot and each had a Lab and they told Jim that they only retrieved about half of what they shot. I don't think it was only at the power line, I think it was all along this stretch of road.

Talked to my brother-in-law today, he worked for Lane County and he operated a blade on Burnhart Rd. during and after the season. He also thought that a recovery rate of around 50% was about right because of seeing a large amount of crippled birds along the road while he was grading.

Don't know how many guns shot this area but it was very popular with the Eugene crowd as they were strung out along this whole stretch of road. Hope this can be of some help to you.

As a result of the 1982 return to a September 1 opening, Bob Jarvis stepped up his criticism of the pigeon's management:

Most of the harvest consists of resident, breeding birds. While Californians undoubtedly shoot many pigeons from Oregon and Washington, it is Oregonians and Washingtonians who are shooting their own breeding stock. It may be appropriate to damn Californians for lots of reasons, but when it comes to bandtails, we are our own worst enemy.

The up side is that if we are the problem, we are also the solution. Over 40 percent of the Oregon harvest is at mineral springs, and nearly all of that comes in the first ten days of September. Hunting the mineral springs is particularly harmful because it selects for breeding adults drawn there by a physiological need—it removes the most valuable component of the population, the experienced breeders.

So, given a different "story line" for bandtails, what kind

of management strategy should we apply? How about the one tried in 1980 and '81, when the opening of the season was delayed two weeks until mid-September. The population index increased dramatically in the two succeeding years.

With such a successful strategy we were on the road to recovery. Right? Wrong! The strategy was immediately abandoned and the population index plummeted to its current all-time low.

I can only speculate on why this successful strategy was abandoned. Paranoia and short-sighted self-interest, the gremlins of most resource issues, probably were at work. Paranoia that those damn Californians would again take advantage of us upstanding Oregonians. And self-interest among hunters who own or have long-term leases on mineral springs (I guess they preferred a mineral spring with no pigeons to one with a shorter hunting season and more pigeons).

There is good news of a sort, however. With the population now down to the crisis level, Oregon and Washington have agreed to delay opening bandtail season until mid-September for at least several years. If the birds fail to recover given that protection, the next step would be a moratorium on hunting them. By now no doubt you have guessed that my story is as much about people and self-delusion as it is about band-tailed pigeons. So I will leave you with this paraphrase: You can fool all of the people some of the time and some of the people all of the time, but the easiest person to fool is yourself.

In 1987 the bandtail population showed the decline mentioned by Jarvis, so Oregon once again set the season back, but only to September 7, which made no difference whatsoever. The limit was cut to four birds per day. In 1988 the season was moved back again, this time to September 15, which aided the birds somewhat. It ran fifteen days, until September 30. In 1989 the season was shortened to seven days, September 15 to September 22. More importantly, the daily limit was reduced to two pigeons per day. That limit nearly had the same effect as a closed season.

In addition, some of the people at the federal level of management began to admit mistakes had been made. In a March 22, 1990, article in the *Oregonian*, Bill Monroe quoted Roy Tomlinson of the U.S. Fish and Wildlife Service: "Pigeons may be headed for threatened and endangered status. We're going to 'do-nothing' them into extinction." Close behind this article, the Oregon Department of Fish and Wildlife admitted that shooting bandtails at mineral sites was damaging: "While from a management point of view it would be desirable to close mineral sites to hunting, mineral sites take such a wide variety of forms that to do so would require individually identifying and closing each known site." But again, that would have amounted to time and money the department wasn't willing to devote. They instead asked hunters not to shoot at mineral sites.

Because of the steadily declining numbers, in 1991 both British Columbia and Washington closed the season on bandtails. Oregon and California opted to keep the pigeon on the legal game bird list but with the short season and two-bird limit.

During this time Ralph Denney had been promoted. My friend Ken Durbin had been successful in filling Denney's vacant job. Ken had previously been a member of the staff publishing *Oregon Wildlife*. He did not hold a degree in wildlife management, and had no biologist training or background. He was, however, one of Ralph Denney's best friends and hunting buddy. Several staff biologists who had applied for the job were more than miffed when Durbin got it.

Ken and I had fished together in the 1970s. We were largely responsible for forming the Santiam Flycasters, a Salem fly-fishing club in 1977. We had dinner parties at each other's homes. I felt sure I could get Ken to act strongly on the mineral spring issue now that Denney was elsewhere.

Again, I was mistaken. In fact, during a visit to his office, he briefly lost his temper when he asked whether I proposed he list all the known mineral sites and create a no-shooting zone around each. To this I answered "Yeah!" That was exactly what I wanted. And before or after this was done, he should print something in *Oregon Wildlife* to let shooters know the harm they had been doing, as Louisa Bateman had instructed the department to do years before. Nothing was done, and Ken Durbin and I ceased to be friends from that day.

When the limit in Oregon was cut to two pigeons per day, for all practical purposes this put an end to legal pigeon shooting. Only a very small number of shooters took the time to shoot just two pigeons. Others, scoffing at such a stopping point, continued to shoot what they felt like. Oregon's game and fish laws are enforced by a branch of the State Police. Several large budget cuts reduced the number of officers in the field and the rest are spread very thinly. Most of their time is devoted to elk and deer enforcement, without much left for species like band-tailed pigeons.

But even after the closure of British Columbia and Washington pigeon hunting and the major cuts in Oregon and California's season and limit, the bandtail continued to decline. Until a few years ago I was both quick and vocal to lay the *entire* blame of the dropping number of bandtails on overshooting. In part, I was incorrect, but only to a small degree.

In the early 1990s an estimated 1500 bandtails died as the result of trichomoniasis in one California river drainage. This deadly scourge to pigeons and doves is caused by the pear-shaped protozoan, *Trichomonas gallinae*. Since there have only been a very few recorded deaths of bandtails from trichomoniasis, all from California, it would be a stretch to speculate that this protozoan has had any noticeable role in the bandtail's decline.

Among those who raise domestic pigeons, trichomoniasis is called canker and is somewhat common. I have several lofts of carneau pigeons, an old breed from Belgium and France that were very popular eighty years ago, now nearly forgotten. Over the years I have had outbreaks of trichomoniasis in my lofts, but it is very easily treated by a host of available medications.

Wild pigeons and doves don't have the same advantage. Especially in the case of mourning doves, trichomoniasis can be deadly as the result of human's good intentions. Doves frequently experience outbreaks of trichomoniasis around bird feeders. The protozoan is transmitted in shared feeding areas or drinking water. It will spread very quickly as more birds become ill. An infected bird becomes listless, can experience difficulty in flying, and most notably, forms an ugly yellow growth that blocks the trachea and oral cavity. The end result is that the bird can neither eat nor, finally, breathe.

A different matter might be the spraying of broadleaves in the Northwest to aid newly planted Douglas firs. Randy Bergman is a farmer along the Columbia River at Clatskanie, Oregon. He is also an observant naturalist and hunter. Over the years he has developed a special interest in bandtails. He, like others, wonders where they all have gone.

The area he knows best is the beautiful Nehalem Valley, in the Coast Range, and especially that part of the valley around the hamlets of Mist and Timber. He has offered to take me into the valley to show me just how much of the elderberry and cascara has been sprayed out.

According to Bergman, "The timber companies began large-scale spraying of broadleaves in the 1970s. In several places everything was killed except the conifers. Some ridges that were once nearly solid cascara back when the pigeons were thick, have none. Today, most of the Nehalem Valley is entirely conifers, very little else. And no pigeons to speak of."

Bob Jarvis told me there indeed might be something in the forestry practices of the last several decades that could be impacting the bandtail. At best, he said he would term it a "suspicion." During his Ph.D. fieldwork, Todd Sanders looked into forestry practices and bandtails. He found nothing conclusive.

"Suspicion," Bob told me. "Maybe there is something there, but we both know what the major problem is and has always been with the pigeon. Shooting them."

I hope that someone takes a much closer look at these practices. In March 2004 I was returning from Waldport, Oregon, after a day of crabbing. As I drove through the Coast Range I pulled over to watch a helicopter briefly. It was equipped with spray arms and was systematically spraying a brushy canyon. It was a canyon with a small creek, just the place red elderberry and cascara favors. It gave me a marked uneasy feeling.

Today, after twelve years of total protection in British Columbia and Washington and a much reduced kill in Oregon and California due to a two-bird limit, the band-tailed pigeon has seemingly stopped its decline. At best it is stabilizing but is still at low numbers. Personally, I have started to see more pigeons during the past couple of years. Apparently, so have some others.

I've heard some grumbling about the "ridiculous" two-bird limit. If the numbers of pigeons continue to increase, you can bet the grumbling will also. Those voices will likely to be heard by those who determine the bandtail's fate. Based on the past, my guess is that the bandtail won't come out ahead from any action they may take. Shooters, public lack of interest in the bird's needs, plain ignorance, all will be faced by the band-tailed pigeon once again.

It's that pigeon potpie mentality.

Bibliography

1949 band-tailed pigeon report. 1949. *Oregon State Game Commission Bulletin* 4 (11): 3.

1950 band-tailed pigeon report. 1951. *Oregon State Game Commission Bulletin* 6 (1): 7.

1957 upland game season successful. 1958. *Oregon State Game Commission Bulletin* 13 (1): 2.

Abbott, Clinton G. 1927. Notes on the nesting of the band-tailed pigeon. *Condor* 29 (2): 121–123.

Adams, Christopher I. G., and Robert Krebs. 1985. First documented record of the band-tailed pigeon in Saskatchewan. *Blue Jay* 43 (1): 40–41.

Alcocer, Figueroa, and Juan Manuel. 1981. Notes on measurements, molting and gonads of *Columba fasciata vioscae. Centzontle: Review of the Society of Mexican Ornithologists* 1 (3/4): 137–146.

Alcorn, J. R. 1941. New and additional Nevada bird records. *Condor* 43 (2): 118–119.

Allen, Walter I. 1941. Nesting of band-tailed pigeon at Altadena, CA. *Condor* 43 (3): 156–157.

American Ornithologists' Union. 2004. *The AOU Check-list of North American Birds.* 7th ed. Shipman, Virginia: Buteo Books.

Anaka, Joyce. 1986. First band-tailed pigeon in Yorkton area. *Blue Jay* 44 (3): 182.

Anderson, Roger. 1992. Band-tailed pigeon at Hawk Ridge. *Loon* 54 (4): 249.

Arnold, Richard. 1979. *Pigeon Shooting.* London: Kaye & Ward.

Audubon, John James. 1827–1838. *The Birds of America.* London: Audubon.

Austin, George T. 1968. The occurrence of certain nonpasserine birds in southern Nevada. *Condor* 70 (4): 391.

Banded bandtails. 1954. *Oregon State Game Commission Bulletin* 9 (2): 7.

Band-tailed pigeons. 1941. *Colorado Conservation Comments* 4 (4): 9–10.

Band-tailed pigeons cause damage in vineyards. 1930. *California Fish & Game* 16 (3): 243.

Band-tailed pigeons destroy fruit in New Mexico. 1929. *Bird Lore* 31 (5): 379.

Band-tailed pigeons destructive to cherries. 1924. *California Fish & Game* 10 (3): 132–133.

Band-tailed pigeons get a look. 1966. *Inland Bird Band News* 38 (4): 77.

Barbour, Thomas. 1943. *Cuban Ornithology.* Cambridge, Massachusetts: Nuttall Ornithological Club.

Barnes, Earl P. 1916. Band-tailed pigeons alleged destroyers of grain. *California Fish & Game* 2 (4): 212.

Bartol, Mary. 1940. High, wild, and handsome. *Outdoor Life* 85 (4): 26–27.

Bartonek, James C. 1985. *Band-tailed Pigeon Harvest and Status.* U.S. Fish and Wildlife Service, Pacific Flyway Council.

Baskett, Thomas S., Mark W. Sayre, Roy E. Tomlinson, and Ralph E. Mirarchi. 1993. *Ecology and Management of the Mourning Dove.* Mechanicsburg, Pennsylvania: Stackpole Books.

Batley, John. 1996. *The Pigeon Shooter.* Shropshire, England: Swan Hill Press.

Bayer, Range D. 1989. *Records of Bird Skins Collected along the Oregon Coast.* Studies in Oregon Ornithology No. 7. Newport, Oregon: Gahmken Press.

Bell, C. C. 1941. Unusual bird records for Kent County, Ontario. *Canadian Field-Naturalist* 55 (1): 13.

Bent, Arthur Cleveland. 1963. *Life Histories of North American Gallinaceous Birds.* New York: Dover.

Betten, H. L. 1944. *Upland Game Shooting.* New York: Alfred A. Knopf.

Braun, Clait E. 1970. The band-tailed pigeon. *Colorado Outdoors* 19 (5): 26–29.

Braun, Clait E. 1971. Bandtails for 1970. *Colorado Outdoors* 20 (5): 40–42.

Braun, Clait E. 1972. *Movements and Hunting Mortality of Colorado Band-tailed Pigeons.* Report to North American Wildlife and Natural Resources Conference, Wildlife Management Institute, March 1972.

Braun, Clait E. 1973. Distribution and habitats of band-tailed pigeons in Colorado. *Proceedings of the Western Association of State Game and Fish Commissions* 53: 336–344.

Braun, Clait E. 1976. *Methods for Locating, Trapping, and Banding Band-tailed Pigeons in Colorado.* Colorado Division of Wildlife Spec. Rept. No. 39.

Braun, Clait E., David E. Brown, Jordan C. Pederson, and Thomas P. Zapatka. 1975. *Results of the Four Corners Cooperative Band-tailed Pigeon Investigation: A Cooperative Research Effort Conducted by the States of Arizona, Colorado, New Mexico, and Utah.* U.S. Fish and Wildlife Service Resource Publ. No. 126.

Braun, Clait E., F. John Ward, J. Allen White, and Robert J. Boyd. 1979. Plumage aberrancies in band-tailed pigeons. *Southwest Naturalist* 24 (2): 391–393.

Brewster, William. 1888. Descriptions of supposed new birds from lower California, Sonora, and Chihuahua, Mexico, and the Bahamas. *Auk* 5 (1): 82–95.

Brock, Kenneth J., and Ted T. Cable. 1981. A first band-tailed pigeon record for Indiana. *Indiana Audubon Quarterly* 59 (4): 116–120.

Brodkorb, Pierce. 1943. Geographic variation in the band-tailed pigeon. *Condor* 45 (1): 19–20.

Brown, David E. 1969. *Bandtail Pigeon Management Information: Period Covered May 1, 1968 to April 30, 1969.* Arizona Game and Fish Department, Phoenix.

Brown, David E. 1970. *Bandtail Pigeon Management Information.* University of Arizona Cooperative Wildlife Research Unit, Bureau of Sports Fisheries and Wildlife, Tucson.

Buller, Sir Walter Lawry. 1967. *Buller's Birds of New Zealand.* Christchurch, New Zealand: Whitcombe & Tombs Ltd.

Burtch, Lewis. 1930. Wild pigeons: Kern County, California. *California Department of Agriculture Monthly Bulletin* 19 (5): 375–376.

Burton, Walter F. 1922. Nesting of the band-tailed pigeon on Vancouver Island, B.C. *Murrelet* 3 (3): 11.

Casazza, Michael L., Michael R. Miller, Julie L. Yee, Dennis L. Orthmeyer, Dan Yparraquirre, and Robert L. Jarvis. 1998. *Development of Reliable Population Indices for Band-tailed Pigeons.* Webless Migratory Game Bird Research Program, U.S. Fish and Wildlife Service.

Casazza, Michael L., Julie L. Yee, Dennis L. Orthmeyer, and Cory Overton. 2002. *Development of a Population Index for Pacific Coast Band-tailed Pigeons.* Webless Migratory Game Bird Research Program, U.S. Fish and Wildlife Service.

Chambers, W. Lee. 1912. Who will save the band-tailed pigeon? *Condor* 14 (3): 108.

Chambers, W. Lee. 1913. More band-tailed pigeon notes. *Condor* 15 (1): 41–42.

Chambers, W. Lee. 1916. Decoys used by market hunters in slaughtering band-tailed pigeons. *Condor* 18 (4): 170.

Chambers, W. Lee. 1936. The hunter in southern California versus wild animal life. *Condor* 38 (5): 199–202.

Chickering, Allen L. 1923. Band-tailed pigeons increasing in California. *Condor* 25 (2): 67.

Coats, Archie. 1963. *Pigeon Shooting.* London: Andre Deutsch Publishing.

Colorado Game and Fish Department biennial report, 1941–1943. 1944. *Colorado Conservation Comments* 7 (1): 23–24.

Conway, Courtney J., and Chris Kirkpatrick. 2002. *An Evaluation of Survey Methods for Monitoring Interior Populations of Band-*

tailed Pigeons. Webless Migratory Game Bird Research Program, U.S. Fish and Wildlife Service.

Cooley, C. Dwight, Jerome A. Jackson, Bette J. Schardien, and Faye Swan. 1979. Band-tailed pigeon, first state record for Mississippi. *Mississippi Kite* 9 (1): 5–6.

Coonrod, Bruce. 1981. A band-tailed pigeon at Pierre. *South Dakota Bird Notes* 33 (3): 59.

Cottam, Clarence. 1941. Indigo bunting and band-tailed pigeon in Utah. *Condor* 43 (2): 122.

Cowan, Lan McTaggart. 1940. Winter occurrence of summer birds on Vancouver Island, B.C. *Condor* 42 (4): 213–214.

Craig, Ray. 1990. Public hearings on draft administration rules for sensitive bird resting, roosting, and watering sites. Oregon Office of State Forester, 6-2-9-452.

Craig, Wallace. 1912. Pigeons do not carry their eggs. *Auk* 29 (3): 392–393.

Cramond, Michael. 1953. *Hunting and Fishing in North America.* Norman: University of Oklahoma Press.

Cramond, Michael. 1967. *Game Bird Hunting in the West.* Vancouver, B.C.: Mitchell Press Ltd.

Culbreath, Jack C. 1946. Colorado's band-tailed pigeons. *Colorado Conservation Comments* 9 (3): 24–25.

Cunningham, Frank P. 1916. Wild pigeons accused of carrying hog cholera. *California Fish & Game* 2 (4): 214.

Curtis, Paul D. 1981a. An albinistic band-tailed pigeon in Evergreen, Colorado. *Western Birds* 12 (4): 185.

Curtis, Paul D. 1981b. Band-tailed pigeon behavior at artificial bait sites in Colorado. *Journal of the Colorado-Wyoming Academy of Sciences* 13 (1): 56.

Curtis, Paul D., and Clait E. Braun. 1980. Evaluation of daily counts of band-tailed pigeons as a census method. *Journal of the Colorado-Wyoming Academy Sciences* 12 (1): 36–37.

Curtis, Paul D., and Clait E. Braun. 1983a. Radiotelemetry locations of nesting band-tailed pigeons in Colorado. *Wilson Bulletin* 95 (3): 464–466.

Curtis, Paul D., and Clait E. Braun. 1983b. Recommendations for establishment and placement of bait sites for counting band-tailed pigeons. *Wildlife Society Bulletin* 11 (4): 381–386.

Curtis, Paul D., Clait E. Braun, and Ronald A. Ryder. 1983. Wing markers: Visibility, wear, and effects on survival of band-tailed pigeons. *Journal of Field Ornithology* 54 (4): 381–386.

Curtis, William. 1971. How to bag bandtails. *Field & Stream* Sept. 1971.

Dalrymple, Byron. 1949. *Doves and Dove Shooting.* New York: G. P. Putnam's Sons.

Denney, Ralph R. 1982. *Band-tailed Pigeon Report.* Oregon Department of Fish and Wildlife.

Derby, W. F. 1920. Band-tailed pigeon nests in Sequoia National Forest. *California Fish & Game* 6 (4): 182.

Drewien, Roderick C., Richard J. Vernimen, Stanley W. Harris, and Charles F. Yocom. 1966. Spring weights of band-tailed pigeons. *Journal of Wildlife Management* 30 (1): 190–192.

Duncan, Lucy R. 1979. A band-tailed pigeon recovery in Florida. *Florida Field Naturalist* 7 (2): 28–29.

Eddy, Garrett. 1953. Winter records of band-tailed pigeons. *Murrelet* 34 (2): 30–31.

Edwards, R. Y. 1956. Band-tailed pigeons and television aerials. *Murrelet* 37 (3): 36–37.

Einarsen, Arthur S. 1936. *Band-tailed Pigeon in the Northwest.* U.S. Bureau of Biological Survey.

Einarsen, Arthur S. 1952. *Band-tailed Pigeons.* Oregon Cooperative Wildlife Research Unit, Oregon State University, Corvallis.

Einarsen, Arthur S. 1953. Problems of the band-tailed pigeon. *Proceedings of the Annual Conference of the Western Association of State Game and Fish Commissions* 33: 140–146.

Eliot, William A. 1923. *Birds of the Pacific Coast.* New York: G. P. Putnam's Sons.

Evans, Maxilla. 1980. First North Carolina record of a band-tailed pigeon. *Chat* 44 (4): 106–107.

Fearing, Percy. 1971. Band-tailed pigeon. *Loon* 43 (2): 57.

Ferris, Reed. 1933. Gulls, murres, and band-tailed pigeons. *News from the Bird Bander* 8 (1): 6–8.

Ferris, Reed. 1944. Trapping band-tailed pigeons. *News from the Bird Bander* 19 (4): 43–44.

Fitzhugh, Lee. 1970. *Literature Review and Bibliography of the Band-tailed Pigeon of Arizona, Colorado, New Mexico, and Utah.* University of Arizona Cooperative Wildlife Research Unit, Bureau of Sports Fisheries and Wildlife, Tucson.

Fitzhugh, Lee. 1974. *Chronology of Calling, Egg Laying, Crop Gland Activity, and Breeding among Wild Band-tailed Pigeons in Arizona.* Ph.D. dissertation, University of Arizona, Tucson.

Fowler, F. H. 1903. Stray notes from southern Arizona. *Condor* 5 (3): 68–71.

Fry, Michael R., and Charles E. Vaughn. 1977. Acorn selection by band-tailed pigeons. *California Fish & Game* 63 (1): 59–60.

Gabrielson, Ira N., and Stanley G. Jewett. 1970. *Birds of the Pacific Northwest.* New York: Dover.

Game harvests for 1951. 1952. *Washington State Game Bulletin* 4 (3): 3.

Gilbert, C. H. 1913. A northern winter station for the band-tailed pigeon. *Condor* 15 (2): 94.

Gilman, M. French. 1903. More about the band-tailed pigeon. *Condor* 5 (5): 134–135.

Glover, Fred A. 1953. A nesting study of the band-tailed pigeon in northwestern California. *California Fish & Game* 39 (3): 397–407.

Goodwin, Derek. 1983. *Pigeons and Doves of the World.* Ithaca, New York: Cornell University Press.

Grinnell, George B. 1910. *American Game Bird Shooting.* New York: Forest and Stream Publishing.

Grinnell, Joseph. 1913. The outlook for conserving the band-tailed pigeon as a game bird of California. *Condor* 15 (1): 25–40.

Grinnell, Joseph. 1928. September nesting of the band-tailed pigeon. *Condor* 30 (1): 126–127.

Grinnell, Joseph, H. C. Bryant, and T. I. Storer. 1918. *The Game Birds of California.* Berkeley: University of California Press.

Hagenstein, Walter M. 1936. Late nesting of the band-tailed pigeon. *Murrelet* 17 (1): 21–22.

Hall, Warren. 1967. A band-tailed pigeon at Spokane, WA. *Murrelet* 48 (3): 57.

Hendrickson, John R. 1949. Behavior of birds during a forest fire. *Condor* 51 (5): 229–230.

Higley, John. 1990. California pigeon challenge. *Field & Stream* December 1990.

Hoffmann, L. E. 1933. Band-tailed pigeons in southern California. *Condor* 35 (6): 232–233.

Houston, Douglas B. 1963. *A Contribution to the Ecology of the Band-tailed Pigeon.* M.A. thesis, University of Wyoming, Laramie.

Hudson, George E. 1967. Common loon and band-tailed pigeon near Pullman, Wash. *Murrelet* 48 (1): 17.

Huey, Laurence M. 1913. With the band-tailed pigeon in San Diego County. *Condor* 15 (4): 151–153.

Hume, Edgar E. 1978. *Ornithologists of the U.S. Army Medical Corps.* New York: Arno Press.

Jarvis, Robert L. 1988. Pigeon numbers plummet needlessly. In *Department News & Views.* Oregon State University, Department of Fisheries and Wildlife.

Jarvis, Robert L., and Michael F. Passmore. 1977. *Band-tailed Pigeon Investigations in Oregon: An Overview.* Report to Pacific Flyway Technical Committee.

Jarvis, Robert L., and Michael F. Passmore. 1992. *Ecology of the Band-tailed Pigeon in Oregon.* U.S. Fish and Wildlife Service.

Jeffrey, Robert. 1970. *Band-tailed Pigeon Research.* Progress Report No. 5. Washington State Game Department.

Jeffrey, Robert. 1974. Letter to W. Mathewson, October 17, 1974.

Jeffrey, Robert, chairman. 1980. Band-tailed pigeon. In *Management of Migratory Shore and Upland Game Birds in North America.* Lincoln: University of Nebraska Press.

Jewett, Stanley G. 1930. An extension of the range of the band-tailed pigeon and of the lead-colored bushtit in Oregon. *Condor* 32 (1): 72.

Jewett, Stanley G. 1941. Late nesting of the band-tailed pigeon. *Condor* 32 (1): 78.

Kautz, Edward J., and Clait E. Brown. 1981. Survival and recovery rates of band-tailed pigeons in Colorado. *Journal of Wildlife Management* 45 (1): 214–218.

Kebbe, Chester E. 1974. Letter to W. Mathewson, October 30, 1974.

Keppie, Daniel M. 1970. *The Development and Evaluation of an Audio-Index Technique for the Band-tailed Pigeon.* M.S. thesis, Oregon State University, Corvallis.

Keppie, Daniel M. 1977. Morning versus afternoon calling of band-tailed pigeons. *Journal of Wildlife Management* 41 (2): 320–322.

Keppie, Daniel M., and Clait E. Braun. 2000. Band-tailed pigeon. No. 530 in *The Birds of North America.* Philadelphia, Pennsylvania: The Birds of North America, Inc.

Keppie, Daniel M., Howard M. Wight, and W. Scott Overton. 1970. A proposed band-tailed pigeon census: A management need. In *Transactions of the 35th North American Wildlife and Natural Resource Conference.*

Kibbe, Bessie W. 1928. Nesting habits of the band-tailed pigeon. *California Fish & Game* 14 (3): 225–227.

Kinghorn, Robert G., and Johnson A. Neff. 1948. *Status of the Band-tailed Pigeon in Colorado, Season of 1947.* Colorado Department. of Game and Fish.

Kloppenburg, H. A. 1922. Band-tailed pigeons abundant in Plumas National Forest. *California Fish & Game* 8: 57.

Knowing the birds. 1946. *Canadian Naturalist* 8 (4): 114–115.

Kraft, Virginia. 1971. Black future for the white-crown. *Sports Illustrated.*

Lamb, Chester C. 1926. The viosca pigeon. *Condor* 28 (6): 262–263.

Land, Hugh C. 1961. Birding on eastern Guatemala's highest mountain. *Florida Naturalist* 34 (2): 65–73.

Letson, Orrin W. 1968. Band-tailed pigeon. *Florida Naturalist* 41 (3): 126.

Levi, Wendell M. 1981. *The Pigeon.* Sumter, South Carolina: Levi Publishing Co.

Lord, William R. 1902. *A First Book upon the Birds of Oregon and Washington.* Boston: The Heinzemann Press.

Mace, Robert U., and Westley M. Batterson. 1961. Results of a band-tailed pigeon banding study at Nehalem, Oregon. *Proceedings of the Annual Conference of the Western Association of State Game and Fish Commissions* 41: 151–153.

MacGregor, Wallace G., and Walton M. Smith. 1955. Nesting and reproduction of the band-tailed pigeon in California. *California Fish & Game* 41 (4): 315–326.

Mailliard, Joseph. 1912. Breeding of the band-tailed pigeon in Marin County, California. *Condor* 14 (5): 194.

March, G. L., and R.M.F.S. Sadleir. 1970. Studies on the band-tailed pigeon in British Columbia. I. Seasonal changes in gonadal development and crop gland activity. *Canadian Journal of Zoology* 48 (6): 1353–1357.

March, G. L., and R.M.F.S. Sadleir. 1972. *Studies on the Band-tailed Pigeon in British Columbia. II. Food Resource and Mineral Gravelling Activity.* Department of Biological Sciences, Simon Fraser University, Vancouver, B.C.

Mathewson, Worth. 2003. *Reflections on Snipe.* Camden, Maine: Country Sport Press.

Matteson, Clyde P. 1952. Pigeon portrait. *Colorado Conservation* 1 (6): 14–15.

McAllister, M. Hall. 1923. The band-tailed pigeon in Yosemite. *California Fish & Game* 9 (3): 99–100.

McCaughran, Donald A., and Robert Jeffrey. 1980. Estimation of the audio index of relative abundance of band-tailed pigeons. *Journal of Wildlife Management* 44 (1): 204–209.

McDowell, Robert D., and Harold W. Pillsbury. 1959. Wildlife damage to crops in the United States. *Journal of Wildlife Management* 23 (2): 240–241.

McLachlan, D. A. 1982. Band-tailed pigeon. In *CRC Handbook of Census Methods for Terrestrial Vertebrates*. Boca Raton, Florida: CRC Press.

McMillan, Ian I. 1949. The concentration of band-tailed pigeons in central California in 1949. *Condor* 51 (5): 243–240.

Mears, Joe. 1949. The bandtails were like bees. *Outdoor Life* 103 (6): 38–40.

Michael, Charles W. 1928. Nesting time of band-tailed pigeons in Yosemite Valley. *Condor* 30 (1): 127.

Michener, Harold. 1936. Band-tailed pigeons near center of Pasadena. *News from the Bird Bander* 11 (1): 3.

Monroe, Bill. 1990. Decline of pigeon population tough issue for wildlife managers. *The Oregonian* (Portland) March 22.

Moran, Nathan. 1919. Nesting of the band-tailed pigeon. *California Fish & Game* 5 (3): 160.

Morse, W. B. 1949. The band-tailed pigeon. *Oregon State Game Commission Bulletin* 4 (7).

Morse, W. B. 1950. Observations on the band-tailed pigeon in Oregon. *Proceedings of the Annual Conference of the Western Association of State Game and Fish Commissions* 30: 102–104.

Morse, W. B. 1957. The band-tail: Another forest crop. *American Forester* 63 (9): 24–25.

Mullen, Floyd C. 1971. *Land of Linn: An Historical Account of Linn County, Oregon* Lebanon, Oregon: Dalton's Printing.

Munro, James Alexander. 1922. The band-tailed pigeon in British Columbia. *Canadian Field-Naturalist* 36: 1–4.

Murphy, John M. 1882. *American Game Bird Shooting*. New York: Orange Judd.

Murtagh, Tom. 2000. *Band-tailed Pigeon Counts*. Oregon Department of Fish and Wildlife.

Murton, R. K. 1965. *The Wood Pigeon*. London: Collins.

Mystery migrant. 1961. *Utah Fish & Game* 17 (2): 8–9.

Neff, Johnson A. 1947. *Habits, Food, and Economic Status of the Band-tailed Pigeon.* North American Fauna Rept. No. 58. U.S. Fish and Wildlife Service.

Neff, Johnson A. 1950a. Band-tailed pigeon banding in Colorado. *News from the Bird Bander* 25 (4): 39.

Neff, Johnson A. 1950b. Matteson tells about bandtail trapping. *News from the Bird Bander* 25 (3): 37.

Neff, Johnson A., compiler. 1952. *Inventory of Band-tailed Pigeon Population in Arizona, Colorado, New Mexico, with Notes on Utah.* U.S. Fish and Wildlife Service, Denver Wildlife Research Laboratory.

Neff, Johnson A., and Jack C. Culbreath. 1947a. Band-tailed pigeon natural history and its value for a management plan. *Proceedings of the Annual Conference of the Western Association of State Game and Fish Commissions* 27: 154–164.

Neff, Johnson A., and Jack C. Culbreath. 1947b. Band-tailed pigeon trapping in Colorado. *News from the Bird Bander* 22 (1): 2–4.

Neff, Johnson A., and Jack C. Culbreath. 1947c. *Colorado Band-tailed Pigeons.* Colorado Game and Fish Department.

Neff, Johnson A., and R. J. Niedrach. 1946. Nesting of the band-tailed pigeon in Colorado. *Condor* 48 (2): 72–74.

Noack, H. R. 1916. Band-tailed pigeons bred in captivity. *California Fish & Game* 2 (4): 212.

Olsen, G. Wilford, and Clait E. Braun. 1976. New species of *Splendidofilaria* and *Chanderella* (Filaroidea: Nematoda), with keys to the species, from the band-tailed pigeon in the Rocky Mountain region. *Great Basin Naturalist* 36 (4): 445–457.

Olsen, G. Wilford, and Clait E. Braun. 1980. Helminth parasites of band-tailed pigeons in Colorado. *Journal of Wildlife Diseases* 16 (1): 65–66.

Oregon Dept. of Fish and Wildlife. 1990. *Oregon Band-tailed Pigeon: Life History and Information.*

Oregon Game Commission. 1952. *Pigeon Shooting Areas.*

Paige, Bruce B. 1964. The band-tailed pigeon in the Panamint Range of California. *Condor* 66 (5): 439–440.

Parks, James. 1973. Interview with W. Mathewson, October 14–15, 1973.

Passmore, Michael F. 1977. *Utilization of Mineral Sites by Band-tailed Pigeons.* M.S. thesis, Oregon State University, Corvallis.

Passmore, Michael F., and Robert L. Jarvis. 1979. Reliability of determining sex of band-tailed pigeons by plumage characters. *Wildlife Society Bulletin* 7 (2): 124–125.

Payne, Robert B. 1969. Band-tailed pigeon in southwestern Michigan. *Jack Pine Warbler* 47 (2): 54–55.

Pearse, Theed. 1935. Display of the band-tailed pigeon. *Murrelet* 16 (3): 71–72.

Pearse, Theed. 1940. Precarious status of the band-tailed pigeon on Vancouver Island. *Murrelet* 21 (11): 10–11.

Pearson, T. Gilbert, editor. 1917. *Birds of America.* Garden City, New York: Garden City Publishing Co.

Peeters, Hans J. 1962. Nuptial behavior of the band-tailed pigeon in the San Francisco Bay area. *Condor* 64 (6): 445–470.

Pierce, Wright M. 1913. Nesting of the band-tailed pigeon. *Condor* 15 (6): 227.

Pigeon banding. 1945. *Eastern Bird Band News* 7 (1): 7.

Prill, A. G. 1893. Band-tailed pigeon. *Oologist* 10 (4): 113–114.

Prill, A. G. 1922. Band-tailed pigeon. *Oologist* 39 (6): 93.

Reed, Chester A. 1965. *North American Bird Eggs.* New York: Dover.

Reeves, Henry M. 1975. *A Contribution to an Annotated Bibliography of North American Cranes, Rails, Woodcock, Snipe, Doves, and Pigeons.* U.S. Fish and Wildlife Service.

Renaud, Wayne. 1970. First sight record of the band-tailed pigeon in Saskatchewan. *Blue Jay* 28 (4).

Robertson, Hugh A. 1988. Relationships between body weight, egg weight, and clutch size in pigeons and doves. *Journal of Zoology (London)* 215 (2): 217–229.

Rogers, Reginald. 1907. Band-tailed pigeons at Santa Clara. *Condor* 9 (1): 28.

Ross, Roland Case. 1934. An aged band-tailed pigeon. *Condor* 36 (1): 42.

Rowley, J. Stuart. 1934. Notes on the nesting of the band-tailed pigeon. *Condor* 36 (5): 216–217.

Sanders, Todd A. 1999. *Habitat Availability, Dietary Mineral Supplement, and Measuring Abundance of Band-Tailed Pigeons in Western Oregon.* Ph.D. dissertation, Oregon State University, Corvallis.

Sanders, Todd A., and Robert A. Jarvis. 1997. *Effect of Habitat Alteration on the Pacific Coast Band-tailed Pigeon Population in Oregon.* Webless Migratory Game Bird Research Program, U.S. Fish and Wildlife Service.

Sanders, Todd A., and Robert A. Jarvis. 1998. *Habitat Analysis of the Pacific Coast Band-tailed Pigeon Population in the Central Coast Range of Oregon.* Webless Migratory Game Bird Research Program, U.S. Fish and Wildlife Service.

Sanders, Todd A., and Robert A. Jarvis. 2000. Do band-tailed pigeons seek a calcium supplement at mineral sites? *Condor* 102: 855–863.

Sanders, Todd A., and Robert A. Jarvis. 2003. Band-tailed pigeon distribution and habitat component availability in western Oregon. *Northwest Science* 77 (3).

Sanderson, Glen C. 1980. *Management of Migratory Shore and Upland Game Birds in North America.* University of Nebraska Press, Lincoln.

Sands, James L. 1969. The bandtail is back. *New Mexico Wildlife* 14 (5): 20–22.

Savage, Meredith S. 1993. *A Descriptive Account of Band-tailed Pigeon Surveys Conducted at Twenty-Three Mineral Springs and Tidal Zones in Washington State.* Washington Department of Wildlife.

Saylor, Ron E. 2002. Letter to W. Mathewson, July 28, 2002.

Schorger, A. W. 1973. *The Passenger Pigeon: Its Natural History and Extinction.* Norman: University of Oklahoma Press.

Sharp, C. S. 1903. The band-tailed pigeon in San Diego County. *Condor* 5 (1): 16.

Sharp, C. S. 1919. Nesting of band-tailed pigeons in San Diego County, California. *Condor* 21 (1): 40–41.

Shufeldt, R. W. 1912. The band-tailed pigeon in North Dakota. *Auk* 29 (4): 539–560.

Sileo, Louis Jr., and E. Lee Fitzhugh. 1969. Incidence of trichomoniasis in the band-tailed pigeon of southern Arizona. *Bulletin of the Wildlife Disease Association* 5 (3): 146.

Silovsky, Gene D. 1969. *Distribution and Mortality of the Pacific Coast Band-Tailed Pigeon.* M.S. thesis, Oregon State University, Corvallis.

Silovsky, Gene D., Howard M. Wight, Leonard H. Sisson, Timothy L. Fox, and Stanley W. Harris. 1968. Methods for determining age of band-tailed pigeons. *Journal of Wildlife Management* 32 (2): 421–424.

Sisson, Leonard Harold. 1968. Calling behavior of band-tailed pigeons in reference to a census technique. M.S. thesis, Oregon State University, Corvallis.

Smith, Harold C. 1964. Band-tailed pigeon. *Oregon State Game Commission Bulletin.*

Smith, Walton A. 1968. The band-tailed pigeon in California. *California Fish & Game* 54 (1): 4–16.

Stabler, Robert M., and Clait E. Braun. 1975. Effects of virulent *Trichomonas gallinae* on the band-tailed pigeon. *Journal of Wildlife Diseases* 11 (4): 482–483.

Stabler, Robert M., and Mark R. Stromberg. 1981. Hematozoa from band-tailed pigeons in New Mexico. *Journal of the Arizona-Nevada Academy of Sciences* 16 (2): 60–61.

Stabler, Robert M., Nancy J. Kitzmiller, and Clait E. Braun. 1977. Blood parasites from band-tailed pigeons. *Journal of Wildlife Management* 41 (1): 128–130.

Stabler, Robert M., Clait E. Braun, and Paul D. Curtis. 1981. Bacterial disease in band-tailed pigeons. *Journal of the Colorado-Wyoming Academy of Sciences* 13 (1): 59.

Stephens, Frank. 1913. Early nesting of the band-tailed pigeon. *Condor* 15 (3): 129.

Stephens, Frank. 1914. Arizona band-tailed pigeon records. *Condor* 16 (6): 259.

Stillman, Albert E. 1928. Nesting of the band-tailed pigeon. *American Forest and Forest Life.*

Stockbridge, Jay. 1976. The case of the band-tailed pigeon. *Washington Wildlife* 28 (3): 10–11.

Stray birds. 1954. *Texas Ornithology Society Newsletter* 2 (7): 11.

Strubbe, Ernest M. 1969. Minnesota's first band-tailed pigeon. *Loon* 41 (3): 68–69.

Sturgis, Harold, and Joe Pesek. 1973. *Monthly Report, August 16–September 15.* Mid-Willamette District, Oregon Game Commission.

Swarth, Harry S. 1908. Some fall migration notes from Arizona. *Condor* 10 (3): 107–116.

Swarth, Harry S. 1912. On the alleged egg-carrying habits of the band-tailed pigeon. *Auk* 29 (4): 540–541.

Taylor, Walter P. 1924. The present status of the band-tailed pigeon on the Pacific Coast. *California Fish & Game* 10 (1): 1–9.

Tomlinson, Roy. 1983. *Pacific Flyway Management Plan for the Pacific Coast Band-tailed Pigeon.* U.S. Fish and Wildlife Service, Pacific Flyway Council.

Twomey, Katherine. 1981. Band-tailed pigeon at hot spring. *South Dakota Bird Notes* 33 (4): 78.

Van Rossem, Adriaan. 1914. Notes from the San Bernardino Mountains. *Condor* 16 (3): 145–146.

Violations of pigeon law numerous. 1923. *California Fish & Game* 9 (2): 57–59.

Vorhies, Charles T. 1928. Band-tailed pigeon nesting in Arizona in September. *Condor* 30 (4): 253.

Wakefield, Brown. 1973. Interview, October 14, 1973.

Wales, Joseph H. 1926. The coo of the band-tailed pigeon. *Condor* 28 (1): 42.

Webb, Paul M. 1968. *Bandtail Pigeon Management Information: Report for May 1, 1967 to April 30, 1968*. Arizona Game and Fish Department.

Weidl, Donald A. 1982. Band-tailed pigeon near Herbert, Saskatchewan. *Blue Jay* 40 (3): 169–179.

Western band-tailed pigeon on the way to extinction. 1932. *Nature Magazine* 20 (1): 42.

White, J. Allen, and Clait E. Braun. 1978. Age and sex determination of juvenile band-tailed pigeons. *Journal of Wildlife Management* 42 (3): 564–569.

Wight, Howard M., Robert U. Mace, and Wesley M. Batterson. 1967. Mortality estimates of an adult band-tailed pigeon population in Oregon. *Journal of Wildlife Management* 31 (3): 519–525.

Willard, F. C. 1913. Some late nesting notes from the Huachuca Mountains, Arizona. *Condor* 15 (1): 41.

Willard, F. C. 1916. Nesting of the band-tailed pigeon in southern Arizona. *Condor* 18 (3): 110–112.

Wilson, Michael. 1968. New sighting of band-tailed pigeon in Alberta. *Blue Jay* 26 (4): 181.

Wire, Frank B. 1960. Unpublished notes.

Wooten, William A. 1955. A trapping technique for band-tailed pigeons. *Journal of Wildlife Management* 19 (3): 411–412.

Zapatka, Tom. 1974. Letter to W. Mathewson, December 4, 1974.

Zeigler, Don L. 1971. *Crop-Milk Cycles in Band-Tailed Pigeons and Losses of Squabs Due to Hunting Pigeons in September*. M.S. thesis, Oregon State University, Corvallis.

Index

.